MOMENTS WITH GOD
FOR MEN

100 DEVOTIONS
FOR LIFE AND ADVENTURE

Our Daily Bread
Publishing™

Interior design by Michael J. Williams

ISBN: 978-1-64070-172-4

Library of Congress Cataloging-in-Publication Data Available

Printed in China
22 23 24 25 26 27 28 29 / 8 7 6 5 4 3 2

INTRODUCTION

L ife is an adventure. Even when you don't want it to be.

You sign your ten-year-old son up for baseball, and before you know it, you're the coach. And now you have to teach eighteen kiddos of varying skills and interest how to field ground balls, run the bases, not be scared to death of pitches, and understand the infield fly rule. And that's just practice.

The games arrive, and you suddenly realize rightfielders like to pick dandelions, third basemen don't know you're not supposed to stand on the bag all the time, and nobody ever knows how many outs there are.

And that's just one tiny part of the adventure.

There's your job, which demands more and more time every day. Your house, which never ends up looking like a Chip and Joanna Gaines reveal no matter how hard you work. And there's the rest of your family, which you're in crazy love with but you wish ran smoothly at least once a week.

And that beautiful woman you married—the love of your life. You'd do anything just to have a few minutes of uninterrupted time with her. Schedule that for about fifteen years from now.

Single guys don't miss out on the adventure. The dating scene probably has a good bit of drama attached. Expectations from family, church, and others are always there because, after all, you have all this free time to move their furniture, fix their cars, and maybe even roof their houses. The adventures are as prevalent as the number of friends you have ("Hey, let's go hike the Appalachian Trail this weekend"), and sometimes you'd like to just turn off your phone and watch an old *Psych* episode.

So, it's not our goal to make your adventure more complicated by thrusting the heavy assignment of reading a devotional book on you. It is our goal with this book, though, to invite you to include the calming, loving, caring presence of Jesus Christ to help you work through your adventures and to make sure your life has the value that gives meaning to everything you do.

We've carefully chosen the articles in this book to guide you toward some vital things you can do to draw you closer to Jesus in a twenty-first-century way.

Two thousand years ago, twelve men had the amazing opportunity to travel the dusty roads of Israel with Jesus—experiencing first-hand the adventures of the Man from Galilee who healed sick people, raised others from the dead, and forgave sins.

That had to be the greatest adventure anyone has ever experienced! Imagine hanging out with the Creator of the universe as the crowds clamored around Him and sat at rapt attention as He spoke.

If you have trusted this Man—this God-man—as your Savior, that adventure is not over. Still today, you can experience Him in fresh, new, and exciting ways.

The articles in this book are designed to help you know the adventure of following Him and living for Him today. For instance, the articles will encourage you to read the Bible, find fellow Christians to worship and serve with, and look for opportunities to serve Him—among other things.

We want you to enjoy a life full of Moments with God—times when you can think about Him, love Him, and worship Him.

So, take some time between sports practices or taking your kids to the zoo or working hard at your job or stealing some time with your wife or playing golf with your buddies to concentrate on the One who cared enough for you to give you an eternity with himself.

You'll discover that those Moments with God will make all of life more valuable and more full of meaning than ever before.

Dave Branon
General Editor
Moments with God for Men

1

See You Next Time

1 Chronicles 16:23–36

Sing to the Lord, all the earth; proclaim
his salvation day after day.

1 Chronicles 16:23

It was a Sunday afternoon several years ago. The whole family was gathered around the table for dinner. The five-year-old son led off the pre-meal prayer: "Dear heavenly Father, thank you for this nice day. Thank you that we could go to church and Sunday school today." Then, to the family's surprise, he ended with, "And we'll see you again next week."

What that kiddo said in his prayer is how we often view the Christian life. We easily fall into a see-you-next-time attitude about God. We forget about Him as we fulfill our daily responsibilities. We go for days at a time trying to pay the bills, keep the boss happy, and give attention to each family member. But we neglect to give God the time He deserves.

First Chronicles 16 gives us some facts about God's power and majesty that we can think and talk about "day after day" (v. 23). We can "declare his glory" (v. 24) and recognize His hand of creation in the heavens (v. 26). We can talk of His honor and majesty, the strength He possesses, and the gladness He gives us (v. 27).

Each day brings new reasons to pray to God, to praise His name, and to proclaim His love. Let's make our worship of Him something we do "day after day."

LIFE MOMENT

Pick a day of the week: Tuesday, let's say. How many fewer times do you think of, talk to, read about, or sing about God on Tuesday than you do on Sunday? Is there any way to change that?

GOD MOMENT

While we set aside Sunday as the Lord's Day, God expects us to use every day to worship Him. Think of three fresh ways to worship Him during the week.

> *Each day brings new reasons to pray to God, to praise His name, and to proclaim His love.*

2

Longing for God

Nehemiah 1:5–11

Even if your exiled people are at the farthest
horizon, I will gather them from there and
bring them to the place I have chosen.

Nehemiah 1:9

When Conner and Sarah Smith moved five miles up the road, their cat S'mores expressed his displeasure by running away. One day Sarah saw a current photo of their old farmhouse on social media. There was S'mores in the picture!

Happily, the Smiths went to retrieve him. S'mores ran away again. Guess where he went? This time, the family who had purchased their house agreed to keep S'mores too. The Smiths couldn't stop the inevitable; S'mores would always return "home."

Nehemiah served in a prestigious position in the king's court in Susa, which was in Babylon, but his heart was elsewhere. He had just heard news of the sad condition of Jerusalem, "the city where my ancestors are buried" (Nehemiah 2:3). And so he prayed, "Remember the instruction you gave your servant Moses, . . . 'if you return to me and obey my commands, then even if your exiled people are at the farthest horizon, I will gather them from there and bring them to the place I have chosen as a dwelling for my Name'" (1:8–9).

Home is where the heart is, they say. In Nehemiah's case, longing for home was more than being tied to the land. It was communion with God that he most desired. Jerusalem was "the place I have chosen as a dwelling for my Name."

LIFE MOMENT

What is the best memory you have of a home where you once lived— perhaps your "growing up" home?

GOD MOMENT

What events in your life make you long for God? Is it at church when you listen to God's Word being taught? Is it listening to Christian music on your truck's radio? Or something else?

> *It was communion with God that Nehemiah most desired.*

3

Beyond Amazing

Psalm 19:1-6

The heavens are the work of your hands.

Psalm 102:25

In 1977, the United States launched a rocket into space. On board was a small craft called *Voyager I*, a probe that was designed to explore the outer planets of our solar system. After *Voyager I* was done sending back photos and data from Jupiter and its neighbors, it didn't stop working. It just kept going.

Today, more than forty-five years later, that tiny vehicle is still going—traveling at a speed of over 38,000 miles per hour. And it's approximately fifteen billion miles from the sun! That's mind-boggling! Brilliant scientists have sent a ship that has crossed into interstellar space. It's astounding. It's amazing.

But it's absolutely puny when compared with what God has done. This is like hearing someone brag to the architect of the Empire State Building that he had traveled to the second floor in an elevator.

We have barely begun to explore the vastness of God's creation. But every small step by mankind should continue to put us in absolute awe of God's power and creativity. Think of this: While we have left the realm of one star with a spaceship, the Creator of the stars "calls forth each of them by name" (Isaiah 40:26). After all, He made them.

Exploring the universe is amazing. But exploring the God who made it all? That's beyond amazing!

LIFE MOMENT

What is your favorite part of the ongoing space program—the moon landing of 1969 or more recent developments relating to Mars? Or something else?

GOD MOMENT

What does it tell us about God's creation that mankind can figure out where planets will be in the solar system and can calculate the exact way gravity and other forces will work now and into the future? Does that say anything about an intelligent design of the universe?

> *Every small step by mankind should continue to put us in absolute awe of God's power and creativity.*

4

The Power of the Gospel

Romans 1:1-7, 14-17

I am so eager to preach the gospel
also to you who are in Rome.

Romans 1:15

ncient Rome had its own version of "the gospel"—the good news. According to the poet Virgil, Zeus, king of the gods, had decreed for the Romans a kingdom without end or boundaries. The gods had chosen Augustus as divine son and savior of the world by ushering in a golden age of peace and prosperity.

This, however, wasn't everyone's idea of good news. For many it was an unwelcome reality enforced by the heavy hand of the emperor's army and executioners. The glory of the empire was built on the backs of enslaved people who served without legal personhood or property at the pleasure of masters who ruled over them.

This was the world in which Paul introduced himself as a servant of Christ (Romans 1:1). Jesus—how Paul had once hated that name! Jesus himself had suffered for admitting to being the king of the Jews and Savior of the world.

This was the good news Paul would explain in the rest of his letter to the Romans. This gospel was "the power of God that brings salvation to everyone who believes" (v. 16). Oh, how it was needed by those who suffered under Caesar! Here was the news of a crucified and resurrected

Savior—the liberator who conquered His enemies by showing how much He loved them.

LIFE MOMENT

Was there ever a time in your life when you disliked the idea of Christianity for some reason? If not, why do you think others sometimes feel that way?

GOD MOMENT

Take a moment to be grateful for the "power of God that brings salvation" and the amazing difference the gospel has made in your life.

> The gospel is "the power of God that brings salvation to everyone who believes" (Romans 1:16).

5

All Too Human

Romans 7:14-25

The trouble is with me, for I am all too human.

Romans 7:14 NLT

British writer Evelyn Waugh wielded his words in a way that accentuated his character flaws. Eventually the novelist converted to Christianity, yet he still struggled. One day a woman asked him, "Mr. Waugh, how can you behave as you do and still call yourself a Christian?" He replied, "Madam, I may be as bad as you say. But believe me, were it not for my religion, I would scarcely be a human being."

Waugh was waging the internal battle the apostle Paul described: "I want to do what is right, but I can't" (Romans 7:18 NLT). He also said, "The trouble is not with the law . . . [It] is with me, for I am all too human" (v. 14 NLT). He further explained, "In my inner being I delight in God's law; but I see another law at work in me. . . . Who will rescue me from this body that is subject to death?" (vv. 22–24). And then the exultant answer: "Thanks be to God, who delivers me through Jesus Christ our Lord!" (v. 25).

When we come in faith to Christ, admitting our wrongdoing and need of a Savior, we immediately become a new creation. But our spiritual formation remains a lifelong journey. As John the disciple observed: "Now we are children of God, and what we will be has not yet been made known. But . . . when Christ appears, we shall be like him, for we shall see him as he is" (1 John 3:2).

LIFE MOMENT

Has anyone ever said to you, "How can you do/say that and call yourself a Christian?" Was that a learning experience or did it just make you upset?

GOD MOMENT

Our efforts are weak in trying to be the kind of Christian we should be. What do you find is most helpful in steering you toward being the person you want to be in Christ?

> *Our spiritual formation remains
> a lifelong journey.*

6

God Hears Everything

1 Kings 18:25-27, 30-38

Let it be known today that you are God.

1 Kings 18:36

One of the longest-recorded postal delays in history lasted eighty-nine years. In 2008 a homeowner in the UK received a party invitation originally mailed in 1919 to a former resident of her address. The note was placed in her mailbox via the Royal Mail, but the reason behind its long delay remains a mystery.

Even the best human efforts at communication sometimes let us down, but Scripture clearly tells us that God never fails to hear His faithful people. In 1 Kings 18, Elijah demonstrated the striking contrast between the pagan god Baal and Jehovah God. In a showdown to demonstrate who the true God was, after Baal's prophets had prayed for hours, Elijah taunted them: "Shout louder! . . . Surely he is a god! Perhaps he is deep in thought, or busy, or traveling. Maybe he is sleeping and must be awakened" (v. 27). Then Elijah prayed for Jehovah to answer so His people might return to faith, and God's power was clearly displayed.

While our prayers may not always be answered as immediately as Elijah's was, or as dramatically, we can be assured that God hears them (Psalm 34:17). The Bible reminds us that He treasures our prayers so much that He keeps them before Him in "golden bowls," like precious incense (Revelation 5:8). God will answer every prayer in His own perfect wisdom and way. There are no lost letters in heaven.

LIFE MOMENT

How do you feel if you message someone, and the recipient doesn't get back to you right away? We love instantaneous responses.

GOD MOMENT

What have you been praying about recently that God is not answering? What do you know about God's responses to prayer in Scripture that can help you as you wait? Perhaps do a search of "prayer" in the Bible to see what you can learn.

> *God will answer every prayer in His own perfect wisdom and way.*

7

Routinely Fresh

Ecclesiastes 1:1–9

What has been done will be done again;
there is nothing new under the sun.

Ecclesiastes 1:9

All of us are bound to repeat ourselves as we go about our daily routine. Time after time we do the same thing: eat, sleep, work, and clean up. We can lose our enthusiasm for life if "there is nothing new under the sun" (Ecclesiastes 1:9).

There's another way to view life, however. Think of the world as a stage on which the drama of eternity is being unfolded. We are the actors. The sun rises and falls like a great curtain day after day, and every time we "repeat our lines" we make a decision. We either respond to the cues of our daily circumstances just to get our part over with, or we look at our role in life as a wonderful opportunity to know and enjoy the goodness and wisdom of the great Director (5:18–20; 12:13–14).

As we gladly participate in this repetitive activity, character is formed, faith is strengthened, hope is increased, and endurance is developed. Through the normal course of events, God is saying to us that there is more to our earthly existence than the meaningless round of duties.

Part of God's plan for us is that we yield to His guidance in ordinary events that occur over and over again. Repeatedly trusting the Lord throughout this month, this week, this day, and this hour is by far the surest way to make life routinely fresh.

LIFE MOMENT

What parts of life seem monotonous to you—to be meaningless repetition of unimportant matters?

GOD MOMENT

Think through your ordinary events of a recent day. In how many of those situations did you acknowledge God and His role? Is a change needed?

> *There is more to our earthly existence than the meaningless round of duties.*

8

Straight Ahead

2 Kings 22:1-2, 8-13

He did what was right in the eyes of the LORD . . . ,
not turning aside to the right or to the left.

2 Kings 22:2

It used to take the steady eye and the firm hand of a farmer to drive a tractor or combine down straight rows. But even the best eyes would overlap rows, and by end of day even the strongest hands would be fatigued. But now there's autosteer—a GPS-based technology that allows for accuracy to within one inch when planting, cultivating, and spraying. It's incredibly efficient and hands-free. Just imagine sitting in a mammoth combine and instead of gripping the wheel, you're gripping a roast beef sandwich. Autosteer is an amazing tool to keep the farmer moving straight ahead.

You may recall the name Josiah. He was crowned king when he was only "eight years old" (2 Kings 22:1). Years later, when Josiah was in his mid-twenties, Hilkiah the high priest found "the Book of the Law" in the temple (v. 8). It was then read to the young king, who tore his robes in sorrow due to his ancestors' disobedience to God. Josiah set about to do what was "right in the eyes of the LORD" (v. 2). The book became a tool to steer the people so there would be no turning to the right or left. God's instructions were there to set things straight.

Allowing the Scriptures to guide us day by day keeps our lives in line with knowing God and His will. The Bible is an amazing tool that, if followed, keeps us moving straight ahead.

LIFE MOMENT

What favorite passage of Scripture do you or could you use as your daily guide? Maybe you have more than one.

GOD MOMENT

"Dear Lord, help me to become so familiar with your Word that I can allow it to guide all of my decisions."

> *Allowing the Scriptures to guide us day by day keeps our lives in line with knowing God and His will.*

9

A Tender and Mighty God

Psalm 147:1–5

[God] heals the brokenhearted and binds up
their wounds. He determines the number of
the stars and calls them each by name.

Psalm 147:3–4

God knows and numbers the stars, yet He is also concerned about you and me—even though we're broken by sin. He repairs our shattered hearts with sensitivity and kindness, and He brings healing into the depths of our souls. The greatness of God's power is the greatness of His heart. His strength is the measure of His love. He is a tender and mighty God.

The psalmist tells us that God "determines the number of the stars," and even "calls them each by name" (147:4). Would He care for the stars, which are mere matter, and not care for us, who bear His image? Of course not. He knows about our struggles, and He cares. It is His business to care.

God, in the form of His Son Jesus, was subject to all our passions (Hebrews 2:18). He understands and does not scold or condemn when we fall short and fail. He leans down and listens to our cries for help. He gently corrects us. He heals through time and with great skill.

The stars will fall from the sky someday. They are not God's major concern—you are! He "is able to keep you from stumbling and to present you before his glorious presence without fault and with great joy" (Jude 1:24). And He will do it!

LIFE MOMENT

What's going on in your life right now that needs this message—that God cares for you?

GOD MOMENT

As strong as we try to be as men, we need God's help. What is encouraging to you as you think about the fact that the Creator of the universe cares about you?

> *The greatness of God's power is the greatness of His heart.*

10

Silent Sermon

Colossians 3:12-17; Hebrews 10:24-25

Let the message of Christ dwell among you richly as you teach and admonish one another with all wisdom through psalms, hymns, and songs from the Spirit.

Colossians 3:16

How important is our fellowship in the local church? Let's answer that question with a story.

A minister was concerned about the absence of a man who had normally attended services. After a few weeks, he decided to visit him. When the pastor arrived at the man's home, he found him all alone, sitting in front of a fireplace. The minister pulled up a chair and sat next to him. But after his initial greeting he said nothing more.

The two sat in silence for a few minutes while the minister stared at the flames in the fireplace. Then he took the tongs and carefully picked up one burning ember from the flames and placed it on the hearth. He sat back in his chair, still silent. His host watched in quiet reflection as the ember flickered and faded. Before long, it was cold and dead.

The minister glanced at his watch and said he had to leave, but first he picked up the cold ember and placed it back in the fire. Immediately it began to glow again with the light and warmth of the burning coals around it.

As the minister rose to leave, his host stood with him and shook his hand. Then, with a smile on his face, the man said, "Thanks for the sermon, pastor. I'll see you in church on Sunday."

LIFE MOMENT

How valuable do you feel church attendance is for yourself? Is there anything about church that causes you to not want to go?

GOD MOMENT

How does Hebrews 10:25 fit into your weekend plans? Does its call to be "meeting together" so we can be "encouraging one another" resonate with you?

> *The coal began to glow again with the light and warmth of the burning coals around it.*

11

The Worst Defeat

2 Kings 25:1-21

It was because of the LORD's anger that all this
happened to Jerusalem and Judah.

2 Kings 24:20

There have been some horrendous defeats in sports history, but none more convincing than Cumberland's 222–0 loss to Georgia Tech in 1916. It was the worst college football defeat ever, and the young men of Cumberland must have been devastated.

Another kind of loss happened to the people of Jerusalem in 586 BC, and it was much worse than any sports defeat. Because of God's punishment for their sin of worshiping other gods, they were defeated by the Babylonian army (2 Kings 24:20).

Led by Nebuchadnezzar, the Babylonians laid siege to the Holy City and left it in ruins. They burned the majestic temple, the palace of the king, and the people's homes.

It was perhaps the worst defeat in the long, often tragic history of God's people. Their continued disobedience to Him had devastating consequences. Through it all, He urged them to repent and turn back to Him.

It's sobering to consider how much the Lord longs for His people to live in a way that glorifies Him. We need to remind ourselves often of our duty to live as God wants us to live because of how much it means to Him.

Judah's worst loss can challenge us all to live in obedience to God.

LIFE MOMENT

What is your worst sports defeat ever—either a team you were on or a team you were rooting for?

GOD MOMENT

If God can rescue His people from the hands of Babylon and a king like Cyrus (see Ezra 1:1–4; also, look up the Cyrus Cylinder online), do you think He can lift you from a seeming defeat? What does that confidence do for you?

> *It's sobering to consider how much the Lord longs for His people to live in a way that glorifies Him.*

The Thinking Christian

2 Corinthians 10:1-11

We demolish arguments and . . . take captive
every thought to make it obedient to Christ.

2 Corinthians 10:5

David McCullough's Pulitzer Prize–winning biography of John Adams, one of America's founding fathers and early presidents, describes him as "both a devout Christian and an independent thinker, and he saw no conflict in that." That's a striking statement, for it carries a note of surprise, suggesting that Christians are somehow naïve or unenlightened, and that the idea of a "thinking Christian" is a contradiction.

Nothing could be further from the truth. One of the great benefits of salvation is that it causes the believer's mind to be guarded by the peace of God (Philippians 4:7), which can foster clear thinking, discernment, and wisdom. Paul described this in his second letter to Corinth when he wrote that in Christ we are equipped to "demolish arguments and . . . take captive every thought to make it obedient to Christ" (2 Corinthians 10:5).

To sift through an argument wisely, to embrace the clarity of the knowledge of God, and to align our thinking with the mind of Christ are valuable skills when living in a world that lacks discernment. These skills enable us to use our minds to represent Christ. Every Christian should be a "thinking Christian." Are you?

LIFE MOMENT

In what ways have some believers in Jesus made people think we can't be "thinking Christians"?

GOD MOMENT

Is it encouraging to you to know that God has equipped you to defend the faith in the right way? Who are a couple of people you would like to talk to about your faith?

> *One of the great benefits of salvation is that it causes the believer's mind to be guarded by the peace of God.*

13

Feeding Ourselves

Hebrews 5:12–6:2

By this time you ought to be teachers.
Hebrews 5:12

The eaglets were hungry, and Mom and Dad seemed to be ignoring them. The oldest of the three decided to solve his hunger problem by gnawing on a twig. Apparently, it wasn't too tasty because he soon abandoned it.

What was intriguing about this little drama, which was being broadcast by webcam from Norfolk Botanical Garden, was that a big fish lay just behind the eaglets. But they had not yet learned to feed themselves. They still relied on their parents to tear their food in tiny pieces and feed it to them. Within a few weeks, however, the parents will teach the eaglets how to feed themselves—one of their first survival lessons. If the eaglets don't learn this skill, they will never be able to survive on their own.

The author of Hebrews spoke of a similar problem in the spiritual realm. Certain people in the church were not growing in spiritual maturity. They had not learned to distinguish between good and bad (Hebrews 5:14). Like the eaglet, they hadn't learned the difference between a twig and a fish. They still needed to be fed by someone else when they should have been feeding not only themselves but others as well (v. 12).

When we get spiritual food from preachers and teachers, that's great! But spiritual growth and survival also depend on learning how to feed ourselves.

LIFE MOMENT

Have you ever watched an eagle webcam (there are many of them) and observed how well the parent eagles care for their young? It's an amazing lesson in God's great creation.

GOD MOMENT

Who in your life have you been able to feed with truths from God's Word, the Bible? How are you feeding yourself on the Word regularly?

> *Spiritual growth and survival depend on knowing how to feed ourselves.*

14

They Never Meet

Psalm 103:6-14

You have put all my sins behind your back.
Isaiah 38:17

D id you know that the *farthest point east* and the *farthest point west* in the United States are both in Alaska? It's a geographical trick, actually. Pochnoi Point on Semisopochnoi Island in the Aleutians is as far west as you can go and still be in the US. But if you travel a few miles farther west, you'll end up at Alaska's Amatignak Island. Because that spot is on the other side of the 180th meridian separating the Eastern and Western Hemispheres, it is technically east of the rest of the US.

But you'll never find a spot where east and west are actually next to each other. In going west, you never "find" east. East goes on forever. West goes on forever. They never meet. (Unlike north and south, which meet at the poles.)

What difference does this make? Just this: When you read in Scripture that your forgiven sins are separated from you "as far as the east is from the west" (Psalm 103:12), you are assured that they are an immeasurable distance away—gone forever. If that's not enough, try this: God says, "I, even I, am he who blots out your transgressions, for my own sake, and remembers your sins no more" (Isaiah 43:25).

Concerned about your sins? Through Jesus's death on the cross, God is able to say, "What sins?" But He will do that only if you put your faith in His Son.

LIFE MOMENT

Another analogy in Scripture for how far our sins are from us is in Micah 7:19 ("depths of the sea"). Did you know that the deepest part of the world's oceans (the Mariana Trench) is more than a mile deeper than Mount Everest is high?

GOD MOMENT

Pause to consider the implications of God's willingness and His ability to forgive sins. That has to have a profound effect on our appreciation of His greatness.

> *When you read in Scripture that your forgiven sins are separated from you "as far as the east is from the west" (Psalm 103:12), you are assured that they are an immeasurable distance away—gone forever.*

15

Run Toward Challenge

2 Kings 6:8-17

He looked and saw the hills full of horses
and chariots of fire all around Elisha.

2 Kings 6:17

Tom chased the young men who were stealing his friend's bike. He didn't have a plan. He only knew he needed to get it back. To his surprise, the three thieves looked his way, dropped the bike, and backed away. Tom was both relieved and impressed with himself as he picked up the bike and turned around. That's when he saw Jeff, his muscular friend who had been trailing close behind.

Elisha's servant panicked when he saw his town surrounded by an enemy army. He ran to Elisha. "Oh no, my lord! What shall we do?" Elisha told him to relax. "Those who are with us are more than those who are with them." Then God opened the servant's eyes, and he "saw the hills full of horses and chariots of fire all round Elisha" (2 Kings 6:15–17).

If you strive to follow Jesus, you may find yourself in some dicey situations. You may risk your reputation, and perhaps even your security, because you're determined to do what's right. You may lose sleep wondering how it will all turn out. Remember, you're not alone. You don't have to be stronger or smarter than the challenge before you. Jesus is with you, and His power is greater than all rivals.

Ask yourself the apostle Paul's question, "If God is for us, who can be against us?" (Romans 8:31). Really, who? No one. Run toward your challenge, with God.

LIFE MOMENT

Have you ever been in a situation where you knew the right thing to do, but in doing it you would face negative consequences? How did you go about deciding what to do?

GOD MOMENT

How does God's power manifest itself in situations when we can't see Him or quantify His involvement?

> Elisha told his servant to relax.
> "Those who are with us are more
> than those who are with them."

16

Life to the Full

John 10:7–15

The thief comes only to steal and kill and destroy; I have
come that they may have life, and have it to the full.

John 10:10

The year was 1918, near the end of World War I, and photographer
Eric Enstrom was putting together a portfolio of his work. He
wanted to include one that communicated a sense of fullness in a
time that felt quite empty to so many people. In his now much-loved
photo, a bearded old man sits at a table with his head bowed and his
hands clasped in prayer. On the surface before him there is only a book,
spectacles, a bowl of gruel, a loaf of bread, and a knife. Nothing more,
but also nothing less.

Some might say the photograph reveals scarcity. But Enstrom's point
was quite the opposite: Here is a full life, one lived in gratitude, one you
and I can experience, regardless of our circumstances. Jesus announces
the good news in John 10 that He gives "life . . . to the full" (v. 10). We
do a grave disservice to such good news when we equate full with pos-
sessing many things. The fullness Jesus speaks of isn't measured in worldly
categories like riches or real estate, but rather a heart, mind, soul, and
strength brimming in gratitude that the Good Shepherd gave "his life for
the sheep" (v. 11) and cares for us and our daily needs. This is a full life—
enjoying a relationship with God—that's possible for every one of us.

LIFE MOMENT

Have you ever seen the photo mentioned in the article? It might be worthwhile to Google it and note the name Eric Enstrom gave to the photo.

GOD MOMENT

Have you been tempted to think that having life "to the full" means that God will lavish material riches on you if you serve Him? How have you sensed the riches of God's goodness in other, more important ways?

> *This is a full life—enjoying a relationship with God.*

17

Wise Aid

1 Thessalonians 5:12-15

Encourage the disheartened, help the
weak, be patient with everyone.
1 Thessalonians 5:14

A t a busy intersection, a man stood beside the road as he often had
before. He held a cardboard sign: "Need money for food. Anything
helps." Drivers look away, as if the man wasn't there. We've all been
there, and we ask ourselves, "Am I the kind of person who ignores the
needy?"

In reality, some people pretend to have needs but are actually con
artists. Others have legitimate needs but face difficulties overcoming de-
structive habits. Social workers tell us it's better to give money to the aid
ministries in our city. We swallow hard and drive past. We feel bad, but
we may have acted wisely.

God commands us to "warn those who are idle and disruptive, encourage the disheartened, help the weak" (1 Thessalonians 5:14). To do
this well we must know who belongs in which category. If we warn a
weak or disheartened person, we may break his spirit; if we help an idle
person, we may encourage laziness. Consequently, we help best from up
close, when we know the person well enough to know what he needs.
Maybe we stop once in a while to ask a few questions of those on the
corners of our commute.

Has God burdened your heart to help someone? Great! Now the work begins. Don't assume you know what that person needs. Ask him to share his story, and listen. Prayerfully give as seems wise and not merely to feel better. When we truly aim "to do what is good for each other," we will more readily "be patient with everyone," even when that person stumbles (vv. 14–15).

LIFE MOMENT

What human need most tugs at your heart and causes you to take action?

GOD MOMENT

Notice that Jesus set a grand example for us by hanging out with and serving the needy people in His earthly life.

> *We help best from up close, when we know the person well enough to know what he needs.*

18

The Leaning Tower

Matthew 7:24–27

Everyone who hears these words of mine and puts them into
practice is like a wise man who built his house on the rock.

Matthew 7:24

You've probably heard of the famous Leaning Tower of Pisa in Italy,
but have you heard of the leaning tower of San Francisco? Its real
name is the Millennium Tower. Built in 2008, this fifty-eight-story
skyscraper stands proudly—but slightly crookedly—in downtown San
Francisco.

The problem? Its engineers didn't dig a deep enough foundation. So
now they're being forced to retrofit the foundation with repairs that
may cost more than the entire tower did when it was originally built—a
fix that some believe is necessary to keep it from collapsing during an
earthquake.

The painful lesson here? Foundations matter. When your foundation
isn't solid, catastrophe could ensue. Jesus taught something similar near
the end of His Sermon on the Mount. In Matthew 7:24–27, He con-
trasts two builders, one who built on a rock, another on sand. When a
storm inevitably came, only the house with a solid foundation was left
standing.

What does this mean for us? Jesus clearly states that our lives must
be built through obedience and trust in Him (v. 24). When we rest in

Him, our lives can find solid ground through God's power and unending grace.

Christ doesn't promise us that we'll never face storms. But He does say that when He's our rock, those storms and torrents will never wash away our faith-fortified foundation in Him.

LIFE MOMENT

What is the worst home repair mistake you ever made? How hard was it to fix?

GOD MOMENT

Underlying God's promises for us is what He did for us in sending Jesus to rescue us. That proves how much He cares, and that helps us trust in a moment of need.

> *Jesus clearly states that our lives must be built through obedience and trust in Him.*

19

In It Together

Romans 12:9-16

Rejoice with those who rejoice; mourn with those who mourn.
Romans 12:15

During a two-month period in 1994, as many as one million Tutsis were slain in Rwanda by Hutu tribe members bent on killing their fellow countrymen. In the wake of this horrific genocide, Bishop Geoffrey Rwubusisi approached his wife about reaching out to women whose loved ones had been slain. Mary's reply was, "All I want to do is cry." She too had lost members of her family. The bishop's response was that of a wise leader and caring husband: "Mary, gather the women together and cry with them." He knew his wife's pain had prepared her to uniquely share in the pain of others.

The church, the family of God, is where all of life can be shared—the good and the not-so-good. The New Testament words "one another" are used to capture our interdependence. "Be devoted to one another in love. Honor one another above yourselves. . . . Live in harmony with one another" (Romans 12:10, 16). The extent of our connectedness is expressed in verse 15: "Rejoice with those who rejoice; mourn with those who mourn."

While the depth and scope of our pain may pale in comparison with those affected by genocide, it's nonetheless personal and real. And as with the pain of Mary, because of what God has done for us it can be embraced and shared for the comfort and good of others.

LIFE MOMENT

What is your reaction when you hear of brutal atrocities?

GOD MOMENT

Guys don't like to talk about this, but we all have painful circumstances that tug at our hearts. What are you going through now, and how does this article help you understand others' difficulties?

> *The church, the family of God, is where all of life can be shared— the good and not-so-good.*

Only Trust

1 Kings 17:8-16

So there was food every day for Elijah and
for the woman and her family.

1 Kings 17:15

Three hundred children were dressed and seated for breakfast, and a prayer of thanks was offered for the food.

But there was no food!

Situations like this were not unusual for orphanage director and missionary George Mueller (1805–1898). Here was yet another opportunity to see how God would provide. Within minutes of Mueller's prayer, a baker who couldn't sleep the night before showed up at the door. Sensing that the orphanage could use the bread, he had made three batches. Not long afterward, the town milkman appeared. His cart had broken down in front of the orphanage. Not wanting the milk to spoil, he offered it to Mueller.

It's normal to experience bouts of worry, anxiety, and self-pity when we lack resources essential to our well-being—food, shelter, health, finances, friendships. First Kings 17:8–16 reminds us that God's help can come through unexpected sources like a needy widow. "I don't have any bread—only a handful of flour in a jar and a little olive oil in a jug" (v. 12). Earlier it was a raven that provided for Elijah (vv. 4–6).

Concerns for our needs to be met can send us searching in many directions. A clear vision of God as the Provider who has promised to supply our needs can be liberating. Before we seek solutions, let's seek Him first. That can save us time, energy, and frustration.

LIFE MOMENT

Have you ever faced a situation when you had no obvious resources and you needed to depend on God to provide? How did He?

GOD MOMENT

What happened with Elijah and the woman was clearly a miracle. Do you think the food arriving for Mueller was a miracle? Why or why not?

> *God's help can come through unexpected sources.*

21

The Jesus Label

Colossians 3:12–17

Whatever you do, whether in word or deed,
do it all in the name of the Lord Jesus.

Colossians 3:17

"Son, I don't have much to give you. But I do have a good name, so don't mess it up." Those wise, weighty words were uttered by Johnnie Bettis as his son Jerome left home for college. Jerome quoted his father in his Pro Football Hall of Fame acceptance speech. These sage words that Jerome has carried with him throughout his life have been so influential that he closed his riveting speech with similar words to his own son. "Son, there's not much that I can give you that's more important than our good name."

A good name is vital for believers in Jesus. Paul's words in Colossians 3:12–17 remind us about who we represent (v. 17). Character is like the clothing that we wear; and this passage puts the "Jesus label" of clothing on display: "As God's chosen people . . . clothe yourselves with compassion, kindness, humility, gentleness and patience. Bear with each other and forgive one another. . . . And over all these virtues put on love" (vv. 12–14). These aren't just our "Sunday clothes." We're to wear them everywhere, all the time, as God works in us to reflect Him. When our lives are characterized by these qualities, we demonstrate that we have His name.

In prayer and with care, let's represent well the name of Jesus.

LIFE MOMENT

What is the best advice you ever got from your dad or another significant male?

GOD MOMENT

What do people outside of the church think of the name Jesus? How can you help change bad perceptions people you know have about Him?

> *A good name is vital for believers in Jesus.*

22

Giving in to Jesus

James 4:6–10

In the same way, count yourselves dead to
sin but alive to God in Christ Jesus.

Romans 6:11

They call it "The Devil's Footprint." It's a foot-shaped impression in the granite on a hill beside a church in Ipswich, Massachusetts. According to local legend, the "footprint" happened one fall day in 1740 when the evangelist George Whitefield preached so powerfully that the devil leaped from the church steeple, landing on the rock on his way out of town.

Though it's only a legend, this fanciful story calls to mind an encouraging truth from God's Word. James 4:7 reminds us, "Submit yourselves, then, to God. Resist the devil, and he will flee from you."

God has given us the strength we need to stand against our adversary and the temptations in our lives. The Bible tells us that "sin shall no longer be your master" (Romans 6:14) because of God's loving grace to us through Jesus Christ. As we run to Jesus when temptation comes, He enables us to stand in His strength. Nothing we face in this life can overcome Him, because He has "overcome the world" (John 16:33).

As we submit ourselves to our Savior, yielding our wills to Him in the moment and walking in obedience to God's Word, He is helping us.

When we give in to Him instead of giving in to temptation, He is able to fight our battles. In Him we can overcome.

LIFE MOMENT

What is your favorite legend?

GOD MOMENT

What do you think it means that God has "overcome the world" in light of all the problems we see around us? What do you need Jesus to overcome in your life?

> *God has given us the strength we need to stand against our adversary and the temptations in our lives.*

23

Out of the Trap

1 Timothy 6:6-10

I have learned the secret of being content.
Philippians 4:12

The Venus flytrap was first discovered in a small area of sandy wetlands in North Carolina. These plants are fascinating to watch because they're carnivorous.

Venus flytraps release a sweet-smelling nectar into colorful traps that resemble open flowers. When an insect crawls inside, sensors along the outer rim are triggered and the trap clamps shut in less than a second—capturing its victim. The trap then closes further and emits enzymes that consume its prey over time, giving the plant nutrients not provided by the sandy soil.

God's Word tells of another trap that can capture unexpectedly. The apostle Paul warned his protégé Timothy: "Those who want to get rich fall into temptation and a trap and into many foolish and harmful desires that plunge people into ruin and destruction." And "some people, eager for money, have wandered from the faith and pierced themselves with many griefs" (1 Timothy 6:9–10).

Money and material things may promise happiness, but when they take first place in our lives, we walk on dangerous ground. We avoid this trap by living with thankful, humble hearts focused on God's goodness to us through Jesus: "godliness with contentment is great gain" (v. 6).

The temporary things of this world never satisfy like God can. True lasting contentment is found only through our relationship with Him.

LIFE MOMENT

What has been the most helpful information you've received regarding money? What's been the worst?

GOD MOMENT

How do you know how God wants you to spend money? When you contemplate making a substantial purchase, is prayer part of the deciding process?

> Money and material things may promise happiness, but when they take first place in our lives, we walk on dangerous ground.

24

A Friend in Failure

Acts 15:36–16:5

Paul did not think it wise to take him,
because he had deserted them.

Acts 15:38

On November 27, 1939, three treasure hunters accompanied by film crews dug through the asphalt outside of the Hollywood Bowl amphitheater in Southern California. They were looking for the Cahuenga Pass treasure, consisting of gold, diamonds, and pearls rumored to have been buried there seventy-five years earlier.

They never found it. After twenty-four days of digging, they struck a boulder and stopped. All they accomplished was a nine-foot-wide, forty-two-foot-deep hole in the ground. They walked away dejected.

To err is human—we all fail sometimes. Scripture tells us that young Mark walked away from Paul and Barnabas on a missionary trip "and had not continued with them in the work." Because of this, "Paul did not think it wise to take him" on his next trip (Acts 15:38), which resulted in a strong disagreement with Barnabas. But in spite of his initial failings, Mark shows up years later in surprising ways. When Paul was lonely and in prison toward the end of his life, he asked for Mark and called him "helpful to me in my ministry" (2 Timothy 4:11). God even inspired Mark to write the gospel that bears his name.

Mark's life shows us that God won't leave us to face our errors and failures alone. We have a Friend who's greater than every mistake. As we follow our Savior, He'll provide the help and strength we need.

LIFE MOMENT

What do you think has been your worst failure in life? Have you recovered? If so, what helped? If not, who can help you move on?

GOD MOMENT

God has promised "Never will I leave you" (Hebrews 13:5). While that was in the context of money, the principle radiates throughout life. How does that truth help you right now in your life?

> *God won't leave us to face our errors and failures alone.*

Listening Beyond
the Stars

Isaiah 55:1-7

Seek the LORD while he may be found.

Isaiah 55:6

Imagine life without mobile phones, Wi-Fi, GPS, Bluetooth devices, or microwave ovens. That's the way it is in the little town of Green Bank, West Virginia, known as "the quietest town in America." It's also the location of the Green Bank Observatory, the world's largest steerable radio telescope. The telescope needs "quiet" to "listen" to naturally occurring radio waves emitted by the movement of pulsars and galaxies in deep space. It has a surface area larger than a football field and stands in the center of the National Radio Quiet Zone, a thirteen-thousand-square-mile area established to prevent electronic interference to the telescope's extreme sensitivity.

This intentional quiet enables scientists to hear "the music of the spheres." It also can remind us of our need to quiet ourselves enough to listen to the One who created the universe. God communicated to a wayward and distracted people through the prophet Isaiah, "Give ear and come to me; listen, that you may live. I will make an everlasting covenant with you" (Isaiah 55:3). God promises His faithful love to all who will seek Him and turn to Him for forgiveness.

We listen intentionally to God by turning from our distractions to meet Him in Scripture and in prayer. God isn't distant. He longs for us to make time for Him so He can be the priority of our daily lives and then for eternity.

LIFE MOMENT

When you have some time to yourself, what do you listen to mostly? Sports? Music? Podcasts? Politics?

GOD MOMENT

How do we actually listen to God? What does that mean? How can you find more time to cultivate the discipline of seeking God?

> *We listen intentionally to God by turning from our distractions to meet Him in Scripture and in prayer.*

26

Living God's Story

Romans 13:8-14

The night is nearly over; the day is almost here.

Romans 13:12

Ernest Hemingway was asked if he could write a compelling story in six words. His response: "For sale: Baby shoes. Never worn." Hemingway's story is powerful because it inspires us to fill in the details. Were the shoes simply not needed by a healthy child? Or was there a tragic loss—something requiring God's deep love and comfort?

The best stories pique our imagination, so it's no surprise that the greatest story ever told stokes the fires of our creativity. God's story has a central plot: He created all things; we (the human race) fell into sin; Jesus came to earth and died and rose again to save us from our sins; and we now await His return and the restoration of all things.

Knowing what has come before and what lies ahead, how should we now live? If Jesus is restoring His entire creation from the clutches of evil, we must "put aside the deeds of darkness and put on the armor of light" (Romans 13:12). This includes turning from sin by God's power and choosing to love Him and others well (vv. 8–10).

The specific ways we fight against evil with Jesus's help will depend on what gifts we have and what needs we see. Let's use our imagination and look around us. Let's seek out the wounded and weeping—extending God's justice, love, and comfort as He guides us.

LIFE MOMENT

Could you write your life story in six words? Give it a try.

GOD MOMENT

In what specific ways can you "fight with Jesus against evil"?

> *Knowing what has come before and what lies ahead, how should we now live?*

27

From Mess to Message

Mark 5:1–20

Tell them how much the Lord has done for
you, and how he has had mercy on you.

Mark 5:19

arryl Strawberry was a baseball legend who nearly destroyed his life
with drugs. But Jesus set him free, and he's been clean for years.
Today he helps others struggling with addiction and points them to
faith. Looking back, he affirms that God turned his mess into a message.

Nothing is too hard for God. When Jesus came ashore near a cemetery after a stormy night on the Sea of Galilee with His disciples, a man possessed by darkness immediately approached Him. Jesus spoke to the demons inside him, drove them away, and set him free.

When Jesus left, the man begged to go along. But Jesus didn't allow it, because He had work for him to do: "Go home to your own people and tell them how much the Lord has done for you" (Mark 5:19).

We never see the man again, but Scripture shows us something intriguing. The people of that region had fearfully pleaded with Jesus "to leave" (v. 17), but the next time He returned there, a large crowd gathered (8:1). Could the crowd have resulted from Jesus sending the formerly demon-possessed man? Could it be that he, once dominated by darkness, became one of the first missionaries, effectively communicating Jesus's power to save?

We'll never know this side of heaven, but this much is clear. When God sets us free to serve Him, He can turn even a messy past into a message of hope and love.

LIFE MOMENT

Is there a Christian athlete you admire? What is it about that person that you find challenging spiritually?

GOD MOMENT

In fact, we were all dominated by darkness until we came to faith in Jesus. Who do you know that needs to hear from you about how Jesus changes lives?

> When God sets us free to serve Him,
> He can turn even a messy past into
> a message of hope and love.

28

No Longer Yourself

Galatians 2:14–21

I have been crucified with Christ and I no longer live, but Christ lives in me. The life I now live in the body, I live by faith in the Son of God, who loved me and gave himself for me.

Galatians 2:20

In the summer of 1859, Monsieur Charles Blondin became the first person to cross Niagara Falls on a tightrope—something he would go on to do hundreds of times. Once he did it with his manager Harry Colcord on his back. Blondin gave Colcord these instructions: "Look up, Harry . . . you are no longer Colcord, you are Blondin. . . . If I sway, sway with me. Do not attempt to do any balancing yourself. If you do, we will both go to our death."

The apostle Paul, in essence, in essence, said to the Galatian believers: You can't walk the line of living a life that is pleasing to God apart from faith in Christ. But here's the good news—you don't have to! No amount of attempting to earn our way to God will ever cut it. So are we passive in our salvation? No! Our invitation is to cling to Christ. Clinging to Jesus means putting to death an old, independent way of living; it's as if we ourselves have died. Yet, we go on living. But "the life [we] now live in the body, [we] live by faith in the Son of God, who loved [us] and gave himself for [us]" (Galatians 2:20).

Where are we trying to walk the tightrope today? God hasn't called us to walk out on the rope to Him; He's called us to cling to Him and walk this life with Him.

LIFE MOMENT

Are there times when you feel that your salvation is a passive deal—that once you're saved you have no responsibilities? What could be the result of that?

GOD MOMENT

What does it mean in a practical way to cling to God? And what does it mean to walk with Him?

> *Are we passive in our salvation? No!*
> *Our invitation is to cling to Christ.*

29

Desert of Diversion

Revelation 2:1–7

You have forsaken the love you had at first.
Consider how far you have fallen!
Revelation 2:4–5

Muynak was once a thriving fishing port on the Aral Sea. But today Muynak sits on the edge of a bitter, salty desert. Sand dunes are strewn with the rusted, hollow hulls of a fishing fleet that once sailed high above on the surface of Central Asia's fountain of life.

Things began changing around 1960 when Soviet government planners began diverting the Aral's water source to irrigate the world's largest cotton belt. No one, however, envisioned the environmental disaster that would result. Weather has become more extreme, the growing season has been shortened by two months, and eighty percent of the region's farmland has been ruined by salt storms that sweep in off the dry seabed.

What happened at Muynak parallels the history of the church of Ephesus. The Ephesian believers, who were once part of a thriving spiritual community, diverted their attention from Christ to the works they were doing in His name (Revelation 2:2–4). They had lost sight of what was most important in their relationship with Christ—their love for Him.

Lord, help me to recognize and repent of whatever it is that diverts my attention from loving you. Flood the desert of my soul with your living water.

LIFE MOMENT

In what way do we divert our attention from the works we should be doing for Jesus?

GOD MOMENT

Is it time to recognize that diversion and talk to the Lord about it?

> *Never lose sight of what is most important in our relationship with Christ—our love for Him.*

30

Tenant of the Tunnel

Colossians 1:1-14

He has rescued us from the dominion of darkness
and brought us into the kingdom of the Son.

Colossians 1:13

For sixteen years, John Kovacs was a "tenant of the tunnel." Along with a few others, John lived underground in an abandoned railroad tunnel in New York City. When Amtrak bought the tunnel and prepared to reopen it, John was forced to look for a place to live above ground.

According to the *New York Times*, Mr. Kovacs became the first person chosen for a new program designed to "transform the homeless into homesteaders." After spending a third of his life in a railroad tunnel, he left his underground existence to become an organic farmer in upstate New York. He was quoted as saying, "The air will be better up there. I'm not going to miss anything. I'm not coming back."

If we could see ourselves as our Lord does, we would realize that every child of God has had a similar experience. We too have been chosen to leave a dark, filthy existence for the dignity of a new life and work. If only we could see our former life as clearly as John Kovacs saw his, we too would know that there is nothing worthwhile in the dark, and there is no reason to go back.

Lord, help me to remember how needy I was when you found me. Forgive me for sometimes wanting to go back to the tunnel.

LIFE MOMENT

Have you ever encountered a homeless person in a way that helped you understand what was truly on his or her heart?

GOD MOMENT

Where do you think you would be if you had never encountered God through His Son Jesus? How different would your life be?

> *There is nothing worthwhile in the dark, and no reason to go back.*

31

Healthcare for the Heart

Proverbs 4:20-27

Guard your heart, for everything you do flows from it.
Proverbs 4:23

I f you're over thirty years old, your heart has already beat more than 1.3 billion times. We all know that when our heart stops beating, it will be too late to change our ways. Perhaps we've been trying to control our weight, get exercise, and watch not only what we eat but also what's eating us.

This last point relates to another vital organ called "the heart"—our spiritual heart. It too has throbbed millions of times with thoughts, affections, and choices. In the heart we determine how we will speak, behave, and respond to life's circumstances (Proverbs 4:23). Will we trust the Lord and choose to be gracious, patient, and loving? Or will we yield to pride, greed, and bitterness?

Today's Scripture reading emphasizes the importance of caring for our heart. Are we keeping spiritually fit?

- Weight: Do we need to lose the weight of unnecessary burdens and cares?

- Pulse: Are we maintaining a steady rhythm of gratitude and praise?

- Blood pressure: Is our trust greater than our anxiety?

• Diet: Are we enjoying the life-giving nutrients of the Word of God?

Have you checked your heart lately?

LIFE MOMENT

How much thought do you give to your physical heart and how to maintain good heart health?

GOD MOMENT

How about your spiritual heart? What could you do to give it new strength with the help of the Holy Spirit?

> *In the heart we determine how we will speak, behave, and respond to life's circumstances.*

32

Flight of Ichabod

1 Samuel 4:12–22

The Glory has departed from Israel, for
the ark of God has been captured.

1 Samuel 4:22

In *The Legend of Sleepy Hollow*, Washington Irving tells of Ichabod Crane, a schoolteacher who seeks to marry a beautiful young woman named Katrina. Key to the story is a headless horseman who haunts the colonial countryside. One night, Ichabod encounters a ghostly apparition on horseback and flees the region in terror. It's clear to the reader that this "horseman" is actually a rival suitor for Katrina, who then marries her.

Ichabod is a name first seen in the Bible, and it too has a gloomy backstory. While at war with the Philistines, Israel carried the sacred ark of the covenant into battle. Bad move. Israel's army was routed and the ark captured. Hophni and Phinehas, the sons of the high priest Eli, were killed (1 Samuel 4:17). Eli too would die (v. 18). When the pregnant wife of Phinehas heard the news, "she went into labor and gave birth, but was overcome by her labor pains" (v. 19). With her last words she named her son Ichabod (literally, "no glory"). "The Glory has departed from Israel," she gasped (v. 22).

Thankfully, God was unfolding a much larger story. His glory would ultimately be revealed in Jesus, who said of His disciples, "I have given them the glory that you [the Father] gave me" (John 17:22).

No one knows where the ark is today, but no matter. Ichabod has fled. Through Jesus, God has given us His very glory!

LIFE MOMENT

Are you intrigued at all about what happened to the ark of the covenant? It might be interesting to read up on the theories about where it might be.

GOD MOMENT

Nothing could thwart the plan God had to bring Jesus into the world. Throughout the Old Testament we see the coming glory. Have you ever thought of how that story thread runs from Genesis to Matthew?

> *God's glory was ultimately revealed in Jesus.*

33

Back in the Battle

2 Samuel 12:26-31

If we confess our sins, he is faithful and just and will forgive
us our sins and purify us from all unrighteousness.

1 John 1:9

A s a child, she had hurled vicious words at her parents. Little did she
know that those words would be her last interaction with them.
Now, even after years of counseling, she can't forgive herself. Guilt
and regret paralyze her.

We all live with regrets—some of them quite terrible. But the Bible
shows us a way through the guilt. Let's look at one example.

There's no sugarcoating what King David did. It was the time "when
kings go off to war," but "David remained in Jerusalem" (2 Samuel
11:1). Away from the battle, he stole another man's wife and tried to
cover it up with murder (vv. 2–5, 14–15). God stopped David's down-
ward plunge (12:1–13), but the king would live the rest of his life with
the knowledge of his sins.

While David was rising from the ashes, his general, Joab, was winning
the battle the king should have been leading (12:26). Joab challenged
David, "Now muster the rest of the troops and besiege the city and capture it" (v. 28). The king finally got back to his God-appointed place as
the leader of his nation and his army (v. 29).

When we permit our past to crush us, in effect we're telling God His grace isn't enough. Regardless of what we've done, our Father extends His complete forgiveness to us. We can find, as David did, grace enough to get back in the battle.

LIFE MOMENT

Seldom are our regrets as big as David's. Yet we have them. What has helped you get past them and move ahead?

GOD MOMENT

Is it better to try to hide your past indiscretions from God or to go ahead and clear the air with Him? We know the answer. How does that happen?

> *Regardless of what we've done, our Father extends His complete forgiveness to us.*

34

True, Deep Desire

Mark 10:46-52

"What do you want me to do for you?" Jesus asked him.

Mark 10:51

A mouse with a shrill voice, Reepicheep is perhaps *The Chronicles of Narnia's* most valiant character. He charged into battle swinging his tiny sword. He rejected fear as he prodded on the *Dawn Treader* toward the Island of Darkness. The secret to Reepicheep's courage? He was deeply connected to his longing to get to Aslan's country. "That is my heart's desire," he said. Reepicheep knew what he truly wanted, and this led him toward his king.

Bartimaeus, a blind man from Jericho, sat in his normal spot jingling his cup for coins when he heard Jesus and the crowd approaching. He yelled out, "Jesus, Son of David, have mercy on me!" (Mark 10:47). The crowd tried to silence him, but Bartimaeus couldn't be stopped.

"Jesus stopped," Mark says (v. 49). In the midst of the throng, Jesus wanted to hear Bartimaeus. "What do you want me to do for you?" Jesus asked (v. 51).

The answer seemed obvious; surely Jesus knew. But He seemed to believe there was power in allowing Bartimaeus to express his deep desire. "I want to see," Bartimaeus said (v. 51). And Jesus sent Bartimaeus home seeing colors, beauty, and the faces of friends for the first time.

Not all desires are met immediately (and desires must be transformed), but what's essential here is how Bartimaeus knew his desire and took it to Jesus. If we'll pay attention, we'll notice that our true desires and longings always lead us to Him.

LIFE MOMENT

What are a couple of the true desires of your heart?

GOD MOMENT

Why did Jesus ask Bartimaeus a question He already knew the answer to? What questions might He being asking you right now?

> *Our true desires and longings always lead us to Jesus.*

35

God's Special Treasure

1 Peter 2:4-10

But you are . . . God's special possession.

1 Peter 2:9

Imagine a vast throne room. Seated on the throne is a great king. He's surrounded by all manner of attendants, each on their best behavior. Now imagine a box that sits at the king's feet. From time to time the king reaches down and runs his hands through the contents. And what's in the box? Jewels, gold, and gemstones particular to the king's tastes. This box holds the king's treasures, a collection that brings him great joy. Can you see that image in your mind's eye?

The Hebrew word for this treasure is *segulah*, and it means "special possession." That word is found in such Old Testament Scriptures as Exodus 19:5, Deuteronomy 7:6, and Psalm 135:4, where it refers to the nation of Israel. But that same word picture shows up in the New Testament by way of the pen of Peter the apostle. He's describing the "people of God," those who "have received mercy" (1 Peter 2:10), a collection that now goes far beyond the nation of Israel. In other words, he's talking about those who believe in Jesus, both Jew and Gentile. And he writes "But you are . . . God's special possession" (v. 9).

Imagine that! The great and powerful King of heaven considers you among His special treasures. He has rescued you from the grip of sin and death. He claims you as His own. The King's voice says, "This one I love. This one is mine."

LIFE MOMENT

How good does it feel when an important person in your life says, proudly, "That's my son!" Or "That's my dad!" Or "He's my husband." Or "He is my best friend!"?

GOD MOMENT

In what ways can it change your life to read this passage every day: "You are . . . God's special possession"?

> The great and powerful King of heaven considers you among His special treasures.

36

Failing to Do Right

James 4:13-17

If anyone, then, knows the good they ought to
do and doesn't do it, it is sin for them.

James 4:17

In his book *Eight Men Out*, Eliot Asinof records the events surrounding the notorious "Black Sox" scandal of 1919. Eight members of the Chicago White Sox baseball club were accused of taking bribes from gamblers in exchange for intentionally losing the World Series. Although they were never convicted in a court of law, all eight were banned from baseball for life.

But one of those players, Buck Weaver, claimed that he had played to win despite knowing about the conspiracy. Though Weaver's performance on the field supported his contention, baseball commissioner Kenesaw Mountain Landis ruled that any player who had knowledge of the scandal, yet chose not to stop it, would still be banned. Weaver was not punished for doing wrong, but for failing to do right.

In his letter to the first-century church, James wrote, "If anyone, then, knows the good they ought to do and doesn't do it, it is sin for them" (4:17). In a world filled with evil and darkness, followers of Christ have the opportunity to shine their light. That often means we must resist the urge to do nothing.

When faced with the choice between doing good and failing to do anything at all, we must always choose to do what's right.

LIFE MOMENT

In the past week, when have you done the wrong thing just by failing to do the right thing?

GOD MOMENT

Why is our behavior so important to God?

> *In a world filled with evil and darkness, followers of Christ have the opportunity to shine their light.*

37

Prayer of the Broken-Down

Psalm 109:21–27

Help me, LORD my God.
Psalm 109:26

Dear Father in heaven, I'm not a praying man, but if you're up there and you can hear me, show me the way. I'm at the end of my rope." That prayer is whispered by a broken-down George Bailey, the character played by Jimmy Stewart in the classic film *It's a Wonderful Life*. In the iconic scene, Bailey's eyes fill with tears. They weren't part of the script, but Stewart later said that as he spoke that prayer he "felt the loneliness, the hopelessness of people who had nowhere to turn." It broke him.

Bailey's prayer, boiled down, is simply "Help me." And this is exactly what's voiced in Psalm 109. David was at the end of his rope: "poor and needy," his "heart . . . wounded" (v. 22), and his body "thin and gaunt" (v. 24). He was fading "like an evening shadow" (v. 23), and sensed himself to be an "object of scorn" in the eyes of his accusers (v. 25). In his extreme brokenness, he had nowhere else to turn. He cried out for the Sovereign Lord to show him the way: "Help me, LORD my God" (v. 26).

There are seasons in our lives when "broken down" says it all. In such times it can be hard to know what to pray. Our loving God will respond to our simple prayer for help.

LIFE MOMENT

What is your favorite line from *It's a Wonderful Life*? If you haven't watched it with your family, isn't it about time?

GOD MOMENT

When was the last time you said to God, simply, "Help me!" Do you think it is honoring to God or pestering to Him if you ask for His help?

> *Our loving God will respond to our simple prayer for help.*

38

Where Are You Headed?

2 Samuel 12:1–14

Then Nathan said to David, "You are the man!"

2 Samuel 12:7

I n northern Thailand, the Wild Boars youth soccer team decided to explore a cave together. After an hour they turned to go back and found that the entrance to the cave was flooded. Rising water pushed them deeper into the cave, day after day, until they were finally trapped more than two miles inside. When they were heroically rescued two weeks later, many wondered how they had become so hopelessly trapped. Answer: one step at a time.

In Israel, Nathan confronted David for killing his loyal soldier, Uriah. How did the man "after [God's] own heart" (1 Samuel 13:14) become guilty of murder? One step at a time. David didn't go from zero to murder in one afternoon. He warmed up to it, over time, as one bad decision bled into others. It started with a second glance that turned into a lustful stare. He abused his kingly power by sending for Bathsheba, then tried to cover up her pregnancy by calling her husband home from the front. When Uriah refused to stay with his wife while his comrades were at war, David decided he would have to die.

We may not be guilty of murder or trapped in a cave of our own making, but we're either moving toward Jesus or toward trouble. Big problems don't develop overnight. They break upon us gradually, one step at a time.

LIFE MOMENT

Do you recall the amazing rescue of the Wild Boars? It was truly remarkable that the boys made it out alive. You can read a recap on the BBC News website: "The Full Story of Thailand's Extraordinary Cave Rescues."

GOD MOMENT

The frightening part of David's story to us could be that he was a man appointed by God and had God's blessing on his work as king—yet he turned his back on God when temptation arose.

> *David didn't go from zero to murder in one afternoon.*

39

Standing Firm

Mark 15:33–44

Let nothing move you.
1 Corinthians 15:58

In the Middle Eastern country where they live, Adrian and his family suffer persecution for their faith. Yet, through it all, they demonstrate Christ's love. During Holy Week, while standing in his church courtyard, which was pummeled by bullets when terrorists used it as training ground, he said, "Today is Good Friday. We remember that Jesus suffered for us on the cross." And suffering, he continued, is something that believers in Jesus there understand. But his family chooses to remain in their homeland: "We're still here, still standing."

These believers follow the example of the women who stood watching as Jesus died on the cross (Mark 15:40). They—including Mary Magdalene, Mary the mother of James and Joseph, and Salome—were brave to stay there, for friends and family members of an enemy of the state could be ridiculed and punished. Yet the women showed their love for Jesus by their very presence with Him. Even as they "followed him and cared for his needs" in Galilee (v. 41), they stood with Him at His hour of deepest need.

When we remember the greatest gift of our Savior, His death on a cross, take a moment to consider how we can stand for Jesus as we face trials of many kinds (see James 1:2–4). Think too about our fellow believers around the world who suffer for their faith. As Adrian asked, "Can you please stand with us in your prayers?"

LIFE MOMENT

We often stand as a sign of respect—standing ovation, standing for the National Anthem, standing when Scripture is read. Maybe that gives new meaning for standing for Jesus in prayer.

GOD MOMENT

Think of what it must have meant to Jesus to see His loyal friends standing with Him as He was brutally crucified.

> *Consider how we can stand for Jesus*
> *as we face trials of many kinds.*

40

In Focus

Acts 3:2–8, 16

By faith in the name of Jesus, this man whom
you see and know was made strong.

Acts 3:16

Author Mark Twain suggested that whatever we look at in life—and how we see it—can influence our next steps, even our destiny. As Twain said, "You can't depend on your eyes when your imagination is out of focus."

Peter too spoke of vision when he replied to a lame beggar, a man whom he and John encountered at the busy temple gate called Beautiful (Acts 3:2). As the man asked them for money, Peter and John looked directly at the man. "Then Peter said, 'Look at us!'" (v. 4).

Why did he say that? As Christ's ambassador, Peter likely wanted the beggar to stop looking at his own limitations—yes, even to stop looking at his need for money. As he looked at the apostles, he would see the reality of having faith in God.

As Peter told him, "Silver or gold I do not have, but what I do have I give you. In the name of Jesus Christ of Nazareth, walk" (v. 6). Then Peter "helped him up, and instantly the man's feet and ankles became strong. He jumped to his feet and began to walk" and give praise (vv. 7–8).

What happened? The man had faith in God (v. 16). As evangelist Charles Spurgeon urged, "Keep your eye simply on Him." When we do, we don't see obstacles. We see God, the One who makes our way clear.

LIFE MOMENT

What life weakness do you struggle with? Do you think the solution is physical or spiritual?

GOD MOMENT

What have you found to be the best ways to keep your eye on the Lord in life's struggles?

> As evangelist Charles Spurgeon urged, "Keep your eye simply on Him."

41

The Way of Life

Judges 7:1–8, 22

The LORD said to Gideon, "You have too many
men. I cannot deliver Midian into their hands,
or Israel would boast against me."

Judges 7:2

In a 2017 soccer World Cup qualifying match that pitted the US against Trinidad and Tobago, the Soca Warriors shocked the world when they beat the US men's national team, a team ranked fifty-six places higher. The 2–1 upset eliminated the US team from the 2018 World Cup.

Trinidad and Tobago's victory was so unexpected in part because the United States' population and resources dwarfed those of the small Caribbean nation. But those seemingly insurmountable advantages weren't enough to defeat the passionate Soca Warriors.

The story of Gideon and the Midianites features a similar upset, one between a small group of fighters and a large army. The Israelite army started with more than thirty-thousand fighters, but the Lord whittled the army down to just three hundred warriors so the nation would learn that their success was dependent on God—not the size of their army, the amount of money in their treasury, or the skill of their leaders (Judges 7:1–8).

It can be tempting to put our trust and confidence in things we can see or measure, but that's not the way of faith. Though it's often difficult, when we are willing to depend on God, to "be strong in the Lord and in his mighty power" (Ephesians 6:10), we can go into situations with courage and confidence, even when we feel overwhelmed and unqualified. His presence and power can do amazing things in and through us.

LIFE MOMENT

What is the best soccer match you have ever seen? What made it so special?

GOD MOMENT

What is something someone has asked you to do, but you don't feel confident? Perhaps a task for your church. Maybe an opportunity to coach a team? Maybe help a friend who is struggling with a moral issue. Do you think God can empower you to act?

> *When we are willing to depend on God, we can go into situations with courage and confidence.*

42

Finders Keepers

Matthew 25:31–40

Whatever you did for one of the least of these
brothers and sisters of mine, you did for me.

Matthew 25:40

People who find something of value are generally eager to keep it. In such cases, the notion of "finders keepers" seems like a good thing. But what if the thing we find is a problem? In that case, we're eager to give it up.

While working for the US Justice Department, Gary Haugen discovered a big problem. *Someone needs to do something about this,* he thought. He looked around for someone who could take on the injustice and abuse of authority he had uncovered. But then he realized that God was looking at him. So Haugen founded International Justice Mission to rescue victims of violence, sexual exploitation, slavery, and oppression.

Just as Moses was God's answer for the slavery of His people in Egypt (Exodus 3:9–10), so too Haugen and his team are becoming God's answer for those in slavery today. As Haugen says, "God doesn't have a Plan B. His plan is you. You are the answer."

God places us in unique circumstances where our abilities match the problem He wants to fix. Jesus said that what we do for those in need, we do for Him (Matthew 25:35–40).

Have you found a problem? How might you be God's solution? God may want you to be an answer to someone's prayer.

LIFE MOMENT

Has there been a time when you found a solution to a problem that had helped a number of people? What caused you to take action?

GOD MOMENT

What has God equipped you to do that can help others? What special abilities did He give you so you could come to someone's aid?

> *God places us in unique circumstances where our abilities match the problem He wants to fix.*

43

Out of Obscurity

2 Kings 22:3-11

I have found the Book of the Law in the temple of the LORD.

2 Kings 22:8

In an old house close to a Civil War battleground in Virginia, workers painstakingly restored graffiti. Unsightly scribbling similar to what we scrub from public view is considered a clue to knowledge of the past. Workers were ecstatic when a new letter or word emerged from obscurity to provide information that had remained hidden for over 145 years.

The story brings to mind a scene in ancient Israel when Hilkiah the priest found the long-lost book of the law in the temple of the Lord. The very words of God, entrusted to the nation of Israel, had been ignored, forgotten, and eventually lost. But King Josiah was determined to follow the Lord, so he instructed the priest to restore worship in the temple. In the process, the Law of Moses was discovered.

But an even greater discovery was yet to be made. Many years later, after meeting Jesus, Philip reported to his friend Nathanael: "We have found the one Moses wrote about in the Law" (John 1:45).

People today get excited about discovering the scribbles of Civil War soldiers. How much more exciting it is to discover the words of almighty God expressed in the Word made flesh, Jesus the Messiah.

LIFE MOMENT

Do discoveries such as the ones mentioned about the Civil War interest you? What era of history do you think would be the most interesting to study?

GOD MOMENT

When do you find the most exciting biblical discoveries? On your own, through your reading, or from your pastor's messages?

> *King Josiah was determined to follow the Lord, so he instructed the priest to restore worship in the temple. In the process, the Law of Moses was discovered.*

44

Run!

1 Corinthians 9:19–27

Do you not know that in a race all the runners run, but only one gets the prize? Run in such a way as to get the prize.

1 Corinthians 9:24

I n the award-winning film *Chariots of Fire*, one of the characters is legendary British sprinter Harold Abrahams. He is obsessed with winning, but in a preliminary 100–meter dash leading up to the 1924 Olympics, he is soundly beaten by his rival, Eric Liddell. Abrahams's response is deep despair. When his girlfriend, Sybil, tries to encourage him, Harold angrily declares, "I run to win. If I can't win, I won't run!" Sybil responds wisely, "If you don't run, you can't win."

Life is full of reversals, and we as Christians are not excluded from disappointments that make us want to give up. But in the race that is the Christian life, Paul challenges us to keep running. He told the Corinthians, "Do you not know that in a race all the runners run, but only one gets the prize? Run in such a way as to get the prize" (1 Corinthians 9:24). We are to run faithfully, Paul is saying, spurred on by the knowledge that we run to honor our King and to receive from Him an eternal crown.

If we falter in our running—if we quit serving God or give in to sin because of our difficulties—we risk losing a rich reward we could have received had we run our best.

Sybil was right. "If you don't run, you can't win."

LIFE MOMENT

If you were ever into running, what event did you compete in? Or if you just watch, what is your favorite running event to spectate?

GOD MOMENT

What does running faithfully for God's glory mean to you? In what ways are you running faithfully? Where is there room for improvement?

> *We run to honor our King and to receive from Him an eternal crown.*

45

What Will We Do in Heaven?

Revelation 22:1-5

His servants will serve him. They will see his face,
and his name will be on their foreheads.
Revelation 22:3-4

One question people normally wonder about is this: What will we do in heaven? Will we sit on clouds and strum celestial harps? Will we flit about on gossamer wings? In his vision recorded in the book of Revelation, John the apostle saw three future heavenly activities.

The first one is *serving* (Revelation 22:3). Perhaps we'll explore an unknown corner of the universe, or, as C. S. Lewis suggests, govern a distant star. Whatever that service may entail, there will be no sense of inadequacy, no weakness, no weariness. In heaven we'll have minds and bodies equal to the task to which we're assigned.

The second activity is *seeing*: We "will see His face" (v. 4). "Now we see only as a reflection as in a mirror" (1 Corinthians 13:12), but in heaven we shall see our Savior face to face, and "we shall be like Him" (1 John 3:2). This is what Revelation 22:4 means when it says, "His name will be on their foreheads." The name of God represents His perfect character, so to bear His name means to be like Him. In heaven we will never again struggle with sin but will reflect the wonder of His holiness forever.

Finally, there is *reigning*. We shall serve our King by ruling and reigning with Him "for ever and ever" (v. 5).

What will we do in heaven? To start with, we'll serve God, see our Savior, and reign with Him forever. And that is just the beginning. Talk about "never a dull moment"!

LIFE MOMENT

What is the most common conception of what we will do in heaven?

GOD MOMENT

What are you most looking forward to in heaven?

> In heaven we will never again struggle with sin.

46

When Life Is Too Big

1 Kings 3:4-14

Now, LORD my God, you have made your servant king
in place of my father David. But I am only a little child
and do not know how to carry out my duties.

1 Kings 3:7

As a young man, Jimmy Carter was a junior officer in the US Navy. He was deeply impacted by Admiral Hyman Rickover, the mastermind of the US nuclear submarine fleet.

Shortly after Carter was inaugurated as president of the United States in 1977, he invited Rickover to the White House for lunch, where the admiral presented Carter with a plaque that read, "O, God, Thy sea is so great, and my boat is so small." That prayer is a useful perspective on the size and complexity of life and our inability to manage it on our own.

Solomon also knew that life could be overwhelming. When he succeeded his father, David, as king of Israel, he confessed his weakness to God, saying, "Now, LORD my God, you have made your servant king in place of my father David. But I am only a little child and do not know how to carry out my duties" (1 Kings 3:7). As a result, he asked for the wisdom to lead in a way that would please God and help others (v. 9).

Is life feeling too big for you? There may not be easy answers to the challenges you are facing, but God promises that if you ask for wisdom,

He will grant it (James 1:5). You don't have to face the overwhelming challenges of life alone.

LIFE MOMENT

What is going on in life right now that seems like it might be a bit too big to handle? What fictional hero would you need to be to tackle this one on your own?

GOD MOMENT

In reality, you don't need to be a fictional hero—you have a real hero in an Almighty God. Have you, like Solomon, asked for God's wisdom in this situation?

> *Solomon asked for the wisdom to lead in a way that would please God and help others.*

47

A Place of Refuge

Psalm 57

I will take refuge in the shadow of your
wings until the disaster has passed.

Psalm 57:1

It is believed that David wrote Psalm 57 while fleeing from King Saul, who hated the former shepherd boy. David ducked into a cave and barely escaped his pursuer. He was safe temporarily, but the threat was still there.

We've all been there. Maybe not in a cave, but pursued by something that strikes fear into our hearts. Perhaps it is the deep sorrow that follows the death of someone we love. Maybe it's the fear of an unknown future. Or it could be an oppressive physical illness that won't go away.

In such circumstances, God does not always remove the difficulty, but He is present to help us. We wish that He would swoop in and whisk us to safety—just as David may have wished for a quick end to Saul's pursuit. We plead with God to stop the pain and make the road to tomorrow smooth and straight. We beg Him to eliminate our struggle. But the difficulty remains. It is then that we have to take refuge in God as David did. While hiding in that cave, he said, "I will take refuge in the shadow of your wings until the disaster has passed" (Psalm 57:1).

Are you in the middle of trouble? Take refuge in the Most High God.

LIFE MOMENT

What is coming up in your life that you are not looking forward to because it scares you? What do you wish you could do? What are you actually going to do?

GOD MOMENT

Does it seem cowardly to depend on God by being under "the shadow of [His] wings"? Do you think David was a coward in this situation?

> *God does not always remove the difficulty, but He is present to help us.*

48

Whodunit?

Genesis 1:1, 20-27

God said, "Let us make mankind in our image, in our likeness."
Genesis 1:26

The word *whodunit* is actually in the dictionary. It means "detective story." The most important whodunit of all time is the question of creation.

Some people wish the Bible said, "In the beginning, God wasn't needed." To those people, it's unacceptable to say, "In the beginning God created the heavens and the earth" (Genesis 1:1), or "Let us make mankind in our image" (v. 26).

Instead, they believe that after an explosion of energy and matter (which itself had no origin or reason to exist), somehow an atmosphere perfectly conducive to life was formed (the chances of that are astronomically slim). Then, single-celled organisms somehow morphed into the exceedingly complex life forms we have today.

No need for God, they say, for it all happened naturally. On an earth and in an atmosphere that had no designing force nor any materials from which to exist, unknown and unknowable forces joined together to place the earth in the perfect spot in the universe and to supply it with perfect materials (minerals, oxygen, food) for life to thrive.

What we do with "In the beginning God" is at the center of it all. We must either believe His Word—and everything His Word claims—or we must believe that our meaningless lives resulted from an accidental, mindless chain reaction. What a stark contrast to the Father, Son, and Holy Spirit saying, "Let us make mankind in our image"!

In the beginning. Was it God? Or was it chance? Our answer to this whodunit reveals whether or not we truly worship the awesome God of creation.

LIFE MOMENT

What troubles you most about the idea of creation as presented in the Bible? What troubles you most about the theories of the appearance of the universe and mankind without God's intervention?

GOD MOMENT

The psalmist said, "The heavens declare the glory of God" (Psalm 19:1). What does that mean in the big picture of creation?

> *What we do with "In the beginning God" is at the center of it all.*

49

God's Amazing Hands

Psalm 31:1-8

Into your hands I commit my spirit;
deliver me, LORD, my faithful God.

Psalm 31:5

Twenty minutes into a flight from New York to San Antonio, the pilots changed the flight plan as calm gave way to chaos. When one of the plane's engines failed, debris from the engine smashed through a window, causing the cabin to decompress. Sadly, several passengers were injured and one person was killed. Had not a calm, capable pilot been in the cockpit—one trained as a Navy fighter pilot—things could have been tragically worse. The headline in one newspaper read, "In Amazing Hands."

In Psalm 31, David revealed that he knew something about the Lord's amazing, caring hands. That's why he could confidently say, "Into your hands I commit my spirit" (v. 5). David believed that the Lord could be trusted even when life got bumpy. Because he was targeted by unfriendly forces, life was very uncomfortable for David. Though vulnerable, he was not without hope. In the midst of harassment David could breathe sighs of relief and rejoice because his faithful, loving God was his source of confidence (vv. 5–7).

Perhaps you find yourself in a season of life when things are coming at you from every direction, and it's difficult to see what's ahead. In the midst of uncertainty, confusion, and chaos one thing remains absolutely certain: those who are secure in the Lord are in amazing hands.

LIFE MOMENT

What life-threatening travel emergency have you faced? How did your relationship with God help you?

GOD MOMENT

What life situations going on right now are forcing you to lean on God in a new and perhaps urgent way? Who do you know who could help you navigate these difficulties in Jesus's name?

> *In the midst of harassment David could breathe sighs of relief and rejoice because his faithful, loving God was his source of confidence.*

50

Great Things!

Psalm 126

> What, then, shall we say in response to these
> things? If God is for us, who can be against us?
>
> Romans 8:31

On November 9, 1989, the world was astonished by the news of the fall of the Berlin Wall. The wall that had divided Berlin, Germany, was coming down, and the city that had been divided for twenty-eight years would be united again. An onlooking world shared in the excitement. Something great had taken place!

When Israel returned to her homeland in 538 BC after being exiled for almost seventy years, it was also momentous. Psalm 126 begins with an over-the-shoulder look at that joy-filled time in the history of Israel. The experience was marked by laughter, joyful singing, and international recognition that God had done great things for His people (v. 2). And what was the response of the recipients of His rescuing mercy? Great things from God prompted great gladness (v. 3). Furthermore, His works in the past became the basis for fresh prayers for the present and bright hope for the future (vv. 4–6).

We need not look far in our own experiences for examples of great things from God, especially if we believe in God through His Son, Jesus. Nineteenth-century hymn writer Fanny Crosby captured this sentiment when she wrote, "Great things He hath taught us, great things He hath done, and great our rejoicing through Jesus the Son." Yes, to God be the glory, great things He has done!

LIFE MOMENTS

What are the Top Three things God has done for you?

GOD MOMENTS

Would you say you have been as thankful as you should be, or do you need to ratchet up the thankfulness a bit for everything God has done?

> *Great things from God
> prompted great gladness.*

51

Free Indeed

John 8:31-36

If the Son sets you free, you will be free indeed.

John 8:36

The film *Amistad* tells the story of West African slaves in 1839 taking over the boat that was transporting them and killing the captain and some of the crew. Eventually they were recaptured, imprisoned, and taken to trial. An unforgettable courtroom scene features Cinqué, leader of the slaves, passionately pleading for freedom. Three simple words—repeated with increasing force by a shackled man with broken English—eventually silenced the courtroom, "Give us free!" Justice was served and the men were freed.

Most people today aren't in danger of being physically bound, yet true liberation from the spiritual bondage of sin remains elusive. The words of Jesus in John 8:36 offer sweet relief: "So if the Son sets you free, you will be free indeed." Jesus pointed to himself as the source of true emancipation because He offers forgiveness to anyone who believes in Him. Though some in Christ's audience claimed freedom (v. 33), their words, attitudes, and actions regarding Jesus betrayed their claim.

Jesus longs to hear those who would echo Cinqué's plea and say, "Give me freedom!" With compassion He awaits the cries of those who are shackled by unbelief or fear or failure. Freedom is a matter of the heart. Such liberty is reserved for those who believe that Jesus is God's

Son, who was sent into the world to break the power of sin's hold on us through His death and resurrection.

LIFE MOMENT

In what way has sin shackled you in the past, and how did it feel when Jesus broke through those chains?

GOD MOMENT

What right does Jesus have to grant freedom to people? Why is He the only one who can do that?

> *With compassion Jesus awaits the cries of those who are shackled by unbelief or fear or failure.*

52

The Triumph of Forgiveness

Psalm 32:1-7

Blessed is the one whose transgressions are
forgiven, whose sins are covered.

Psalm 32:1

Mack, having struggled with drug abuse and sexual sin, was desperate. Relationships he valued were in disarray, and his conscience was beating him up. In his misery, he found himself unannounced at a church asking to speak with a pastor. There he found relief in sharing his complicated story and in hearing about God's mercy and forgiveness.

Psalm 32 is believed to have been composed by David after his sexual sin. He compounded his wrongdoing by devising a sinister strategy that resulted in the death of the woman's husband (see 2 Samuel 11–12). While these ugly incidents were behind him, the effects of his actions remained. Psalm 32:3–4 describes the deep struggles he experienced before he acknowledged the ugliness of his deeds; the gnawing effects of unconfessed sin were undeniable. What brought relief? Relief began with confession to God and accepting the forgiveness He offers (v. 5).

What a great place for us to start—at the place of God's mercy—after we have said or done things that hurt and harm ourselves and others. The guilt of our sin doesn't have to be permanent. God's arms are open wide to receive us when we acknowledge our wrongs and seek His forgiveness. We can join David, who knew what he was talking about when he said, "Blessed is the one whose transgressions are forgiven, whose sins are covered" (v. 1).

LIFE MOMENT

What can we learn about coverups from David's story?

GOD MOMENT

Take a moment and read Psalm 32. When there is sin, there are two roles: man's and God's. What is man's role here? What is God's role?

> *What a great place for us to start—*
> *at the place of God's mercy.*

53

Deeper Love

1 Peter 4:7-11

God demonstrates his own love for us in this:
While we were still sinners, Christ died for us.

Romans 5:8

When they first met, Edwin Stanton snubbed US president Abraham Lincoln personally and professionally—even referring to him as a "long-armed creature." But Lincoln appreciated Stanton's abilities and chose to forgive him, eventually appointing Stanton to a vital cabinet position during the Civil War. Stanton later grew to love Lincoln as a friend. It was Stanton who sat by Lincoln's bed throughout the night after the president was shot at Ford's Theater, and he whispered through tears on his passing, "Now he belongs to the ages."

Reconciliation is a beautiful thing. The apostle Peter pointed followers of Jesus there when he wrote, "Above all, love each other deeply, because love covers over a multitude of sins" (1 Peter 4:8). Peter's words cause me to wonder if he was thinking of his own denial of Jesus (Luke 22:54–62) and the forgiveness Jesus offered him (and us) through the cross.

The deep love Jesus demonstrated through His death on the cross frees us from the debt for our sins and opens the way for our reconciliation with God (Colossians 1:19–20). His forgiveness empowers us to forgive others as we realize we can't forgive in our own strength and ask Him to help us. When we love others because our Savior loves them and when we forgive others because He has forgiven us, God allows us to let go of the past. Then we can walk forward with Him by His grace into amazing new places.

LIFE MOMENT

When have you seen reconciliation with a family member change a negative situation into a positive one?

GOD MOMENT

The key to understanding God's forgiveness is this: While we were still in our sin, God forgave us. What does that mean as you look at your situation?

> *Reconciliation is a beautiful thing.*

54

Alert Circles

Hebrews 10:19-25

Encourage one another and build each other up.

1 Thessalonians 5:11

African gazelles instinctively form "alert circles" while resting on the savannah. They gather in groups with each animal facing outward in a slightly different direction. This enables them to scan the horizon a full 360 degrees and to communicate about approaching dangers or opportunities.

Instead of looking out only for themselves, the members of the group take care of one another. This is also God's wisdom for followers of Jesus. The Bible encourages us, "Let us consider how we may spur one another on toward love and good deeds, not giving up meeting together" (Hebrews 10:24–25).

Christians were never intended to go it alone, explains the writer of Hebrews. Together we are stronger. We are able to "[encourage] one another" (v. 25), to "comfort those in any trouble with the comfort we ourselves receive from God" (2 Corinthians 1:4), and to help each other stay alert to the efforts of our enemy the devil, who "prowls around like a roaring lion looking for someone to devour" (1 Peter 5:8).

The goal of our care for each other is so much more than survival. It is to make us like Jesus: loving and effective servants of God in this world—people who together look forward confidently to the hope of

His coming kingdom. All of us need encouragement, and God will help us help each other as together we draw near to Him in love.

LIFE MOMENT

Who are a couple of friends you can depend on for help—even spiritual help—when you need it?

GOD MOMENT

In what ways is God equipping you to be the go-to guy for others?

> *Christians were never intended to go it alone.*

55

Gardening Tips

Mark 4:1-9

Others, like seed sown on good soil, hear the
word, accept it, and produce a crop.

Mark 4:20

A book about maintaining a good garden contained this great advice: Take care of the soil, and don't worry about the plants. If the soil is good, the seed will take root and grow."

In the parable of the sower in Mark 4, Jesus spoke of the importance of "good soil." He defined good soil as referring to people who "hear" God's Word, "accept it," and "produce a crop" (v. 20). If we keep our heart soft and receptive to what God wants us to know, His message in the Bible will take root, grow, and produce fruit.

When we plant our crops—whether a backyard garden or a huge field of corn—life is in the seed. Under the right conditions, it will grow until it reaches maturity and produces fruit. Similarly, if the seed of the Word is planted in the good soil of a receptive heart, it will grow until the character of Jesus is seen.

For the Christian, the power of the spiritual life comes from the indwelling Holy Spirit. As we open our heart to the Word with an eagerness to obey it, the Spirit causes us to grow and bear fruit (Galatians 5:22–23).

We can't make ourselves grow, any more than we can force growth from the seeds in our gardens. But we can tend the soil, keeping our hearts soft, receptive, and obedient to God's Word. Then we will yield the fruit of righteousness.

What kind of soil are you?

LIFE MOMENT

If you were a farmer, what crop would you like to grow?

GOD MOMENT

How does the Holy Spirit interact with you in your life?

> *The power of the spiritual life comes from the indwelling Holy Spirit.*

56

New Songs

Psalm 40:1-10

He put a new song in my mouth, a hymn of praise to our God.
Psalm 40:3

The song of the humpback whale is one of the strangest in nature. It is a weird combination of high- and low-pitched groanings. Those who have studied the humpback whale say their songs are noteworthy because these giants of the deep are continually changing them. New patterns are added and old ones eliminated so that over a period of time the whale actually sings a whole new song.

There's a sense in which a Christian should be continually composing new songs of praise around the fresh mercies of God. Unfortunately, many of us just keep singing "the same old song."

We must repeatedly affirm the fundamentals of our faith. But as the psalmist tells us, the works of God's deliverance in the lives of His people are many. His works, which are more than we can count, give us reasons to express our praise to Him in numerous ways (Psalm 40:5).

So why do we express our testimony of God's saving grace in the same old way year after year? A fresh experience of the mercies of the cross and of Christ's resurrection power should continually fill our hearts and minds with new songs.

The gospel story never changes—thank God for that. But our songs of praise should always be new.

LIFE MOMENT

Do you feel that you, as the writer says, "keep singing 'the same old song'" spiritually?

GOD MOMENT

What are some ways you can refresh your expressions of love for Jesus? Reading a new book by a Christian writer? Listening to new praise music? Tuning in to Christian podcasts? Further ideas?

> *A fresh experience of the mercies of the cross and of Christ's resurrection power should continually fill our hearts and minds with new songs.*

57

The Beauty of Rome

John 17:1–5

Now this is eternal life: that they know you, the only true God.

John 17:3

The glory of the Roman Empire offered an expansive backdrop for the birth of Jesus. In 27 BC, Rome's first emperor, Caesar Augustus, ended two hundred years of civil war and began to replace rundown neighborhoods with monuments, temples, arenas, and government complexes. According to Roman historian Pliny the Elder, they were "the most beautiful buildings the world has ever seen."

Yet even with her beauty, the Eternal City and its empire had a history of brutality that continued until Rome fell. Thousands of slaves, foreigners, revolutionaries, and army deserters were crucified on roadside poles as a warning to anyone who dared to defy the power of Rome.

What irony that Jesus's death on a Roman cross turned out to reveal an eternal glory that made the pride of Rome look like the momentary beauty of a sunset!

Who could have imagined that in the public curse and agony of the cross we would find the eternal glory of the love, presence, and kingdom of our God?

Who could have foreseen that all heaven and earth would one day sing, "Worthy is the Lamb, who was slain, to receive power and wealth and wisdom and strength and honor and glory and praise!" (Revelation 5:12).

LIFE MOMENT

Of all the buildings in the world, what is the most beautiful, inspiring building you have seen (in person or in pictures)?

GOD MOMENT

Think about this: The most brutal, ugliest torture implement—the cross—has become a thing of beauty to us. Why is the cross such a wonderful emblem?

> In the public curse and agony of the cross we find the eternal glory of the love, presence, and kingdom of our God.

58

From Here to Heaven

Ephesians 2:1-10

We are God's handiwork, created in Christ Jesus to do
good works, which God prepared in advance for us to do.

Ephesians 2:10

Pro athletes sometimes get something for nothing. You might have heard of players who signed a long-term contract to play but were forced to retire before the contract expired. In some sports, like baseball, the team has to keep paying the player. One player famously gets a check for more than one million dollars every July 1 until 2035 although he retired in 2001. And he has to do absolutely nothing to get that money.

We as Christians have to be careful that we don't view our saving faith like that. We must never think, "Hey, I'm saved. I've got eternal riches coming my way. I don't have to do anything for God."

That's partially right but very wrong. In one regard, our journey from here to heaven is paid for in full by Jesus's sacrifice. There's nothing we can do to earn salvation. But there's another part of this that we must consider.

In Ephesians 2:8–9, after Paul clearly says that we do not have to do anything and that salvation is a "gift of God," he goes on. Verse 10 says we indeed have a job to do. As believers, we are "created in Christ Jesus to do good works." God has tasks planned for us to do while we are on this earth—not to pay our debt but to honor our Savior.

Life from here to heaven is not a vacation cruise—it's a wonderful privilege and calling to serve God.

LIFE MOMENT

Sometimes we get a little perturbed by the huge amount of money athletes who are still competing get paid. Who do you think is the most overpaid athlete in sports?

GOD MOMENT

Jesus paid the price for our sin, meaning we get something we don't deserve at all—adoption into God's family, life "to the full" (John 10:10), and eternal life in God's presence. We don't pay for it, but what should we be doing as a way of saying thank you?

> *God has tasks planned for us to do while we are on this earth—not to pay our debt but to honor our Savior.*

59

Taking Shortcuts

Luke 9:57–62

Whoever wants to be my disciple must deny themselves
and take up their cross daily and follow me.

Luke 9:23

Spring rains and sunshine had coaxed a riotous expanse of color from a well-groomed flowerbed of bright flowers. Observing the amazing landscape that held those flowers, someone commented, "I want that look without all the work."

Some shortcuts are fine—even practical. Nothing wrong with figuring out how to get a great yard without backbreaking work!

Other shortcuts short-circuit our spirit and deaden our lives. We want relationships without the difficulties and messiness of committing to someone so different from ourselves. We want "greatness" without the risks and failures necessary in the adventure of real life. We desire to please God, but not when it inconveniences us.

Jesus made clear to His followers that there is no shortcut that avoids the hard choice of surrendering our lives to Him. He warned a prospective disciple, "No one who puts a hand to the plow and looks back is fit for service in the kingdom of God" (Luke 9:62). To follow Christ requires a radical altering of our loyalties.

When we turn in faith to Jesus, the work just begins. But it is oh-so-worth-it, for He also told us that no one who sacrifices "for me and the gospel will fail to receive a hundred times as much in this present age . . . and in the age to come eternal life" (Mark 10:29–30). The work of following Christ is difficult, but He's given us His Spirit and the reward is a full, joyful life now and forever.

LIFE MOMENT

If you could snap your fingers and make one major physical change to your home, what would it be?

GOD MOMENT

Jesus did all the work of salvation by dying on the cross, so what efforts do we still have to make to strengthen our relationship with Him?

> *Jesus made clear to His followers that there is no shortcut that avoids the hard choice of surrendering our lives to Him.*

60

Divine Rescue

Amos 5:10-24

Let justice roll on like a river, righteousness
like a never-failing stream!

Amos 5:24

When John Lewis, an American congressman and civil rights leader, died in 2020, people from many political persuasions mourned. In 1965, Lewis marched with Martin Luther King Jr. to secure voting rights for Black citizens. During the march, Lewis suffered a cracked skull, causing scars he carried the rest of his life. "When you see something that is not right, not just, not fair," Lewis said, "you have a moral obligation to say something. To do something." He also said, "Never, ever, be afraid to make some noise and get in good, necessary trouble."

Lewis learned early that doing what was right, to be faithful to the truth, required making "good" trouble. He would need to speak things that were unpopular. The prophet Amos knew this too. Seeing Israel's sin and injustice, he couldn't keep quiet. Amos denounced how the powerful were oppressing "the innocent and tak[ing] bribes and depriv[ing] the poor of justice in the courts," while building "stone mansions" with "lush vineyards" (Amos 5:11–12). Rather than maintaining his own safety and comfort by staying out of the fray, Amos named the evil. The prophet made good, necessary trouble.

But this trouble aimed at something good—justice for all. "Let justice roll on like a river!" Amos exclaimed (v. 24). When we get into good trouble (the kind of righteous, nonviolent trouble justice requires), the goal is always goodness and healing.

LIFE MOMENT

When have you had to approach others to make a necessary change but, when you did, you were going against the flow—causing "good" trouble?

GOD MOMENT

Is there anything God is speaking to you about now in regard to seeing that people are treated justly—at church, at work, in your neighborhood?

The goal is always goodness and healing.

61

Spending Time with God

Luke 5:12–16

Jesus often withdrew to lonely places and prayed.
Luke 5:16

A *River Runs Through It* is Norman Maclean's masterful story of two boys growing up in western Montana with their father, a Presbyterian minister. On Sunday mornings, Norman and his brother, Paul, went to church where they heard their father preach. Once Sunday evening rolled around, there was another service and their father would preach again. But between those two services, they were free to walk the hills and streams with him "while he unwound between services." It was an intentional withdrawing on their father's part to "restore his soul and be filled again to overflowing for the evening sermon."

Throughout the Gospels, Jesus is seen teaching multitudes on hillsides and cities, and healing the sick and diseased who were brought to Him. All this interaction was in line with the Son of Man's mission "to seek and to save the lost" (Luke 19:10). But it's also noted that He "often withdrew to lonely places" (5:16). His time there was spent communing with the Father, being renewed and restored to step back once more into His mission.

In our faithful efforts to serve, it's good for us to remember that Jesus "often" withdrew. If this practice was important for Jesus, how much more so for us? May we regularly spend time with our Father, who can fill us again to overflowing.

LIFE MOMENT

Where is your favorite place in your house to be alone with your thoughts and with God?

GOD MOMENT

Imagine what it must have been like for Jesus to have spent the day ministering to people throughout Galilee—and then have a time to talk alone with God. What do you think He might have said to the Father?

> *Jesus spent time communing with the Father, being renewed and restored.*

62

Social Stomachs

Ezekiel 2:1–3:4

Blessed are those whose ways are blameless,
who walk according to the law of the Lord.

Psalm 119:1

Honey ants survive in difficult times by depending on certain members of their group known as "honey pots." They take in so much nectar that they swell up until they resemble little round berries, hardly able to move. When food and water become scarce, these ants act as "social stomachs" and sustain the entire colony by dispensing what they have stored in their own bodies.

Similarly, the messenger of God must fill his heart and mind with the truths of Scripture. Only as he is faithful in applying the Word of God to his own life can he honestly give its nourishing encouragement and exhortation to others.

The Lord told the prophet Ezekiel to eat a scroll that contained a message full of "lament and mourning and woe" (Ezekiel 2:10). Because he was submissive to the Lord and applied the lesson to his own heart first, he could boldly present the life-giving message to all who would listen.

As believers, we too must develop a "social stomach" by digesting the truths of the Bible and allowing the Spirit of God to make them a part of our lives. Then, filled with God's Word, we can speak effectively to others who need spiritual food.

LIFE MOMENT

The natural world God created is amazing! What insect or animal fascinates you the most?

GOD MOMENT

How comfortable are you in speaking to others about spiritual matters? If it is difficult, who could help you develop that skill?

> The messenger of God must fill his heart
> and mind with the truths of Scripture.

63

Walking Backward

Philippians 2:1-11

Rather, [Jesus] made himself nothing.

Philippians 2:7

British newsreel crew filmed six-year-old Flannery O'Connor on her family farm in 1932. Flannery, who would go on to become an acclaimed US writer, caught the crew's curiosity because she'd taught a chicken to walk backward. Apart from the novelty of the feat, I thought this glimpse of history was a perfect metaphor. Flannery, due to both her literary sensibilities and her spiritual convictions, spent her thirty-nine years definitely walking backward—thinking and writing in a countercultural way. Publishers and readers were entirely baffled by how her biblical themes ran counter to the religious views they expected.

A life that runs counter to the norm is inevitable for those who would truly imitate Jesus. Philippians tells us that Jesus, though His "very nature" was God, didn't move in the predictable ways we would expect (2:6). He didn't use His power "to his own advantage," but "rather, he made himself nothing by taking the very nature of a servant" (vv. 6–7). Christ, the Lord of creation, surrendered to death for the sake of love. He didn't seize prestige but embraced humility. He didn't grab power but relinquished control. Jesus, in essence, walked backward—counter to the power-driven ways of the world.

Scripture tells us to do the same (v. 5). Like Jesus, we serve rather than dominate. We move toward humility rather than prominence. We give rather than take. In Jesus's power, we walk backward.

LIFE MOMENT

When does your life as a Christian seem the most countercultural?

GOD MOMENT

How does God protect you from a hunger for power when it is service and self-sacrifice that most honors Him?

> *Like Jesus, we serve rather than dominate.*

64

The Tree Whisperer

Psalm 1

That person is like a tree planted by streams
of water, which yields its fruit in season.

Psalm 1:3

Some call him the "tree whisperer." Tony Rinaudo is, in fact, World Vision Australia's forest maker. He's a missionary and agronomist engaged in a thirty-year effort to share Jesus by combating deforestation across Africa's Sahel, south of the Sahara.

Realizing stunted "shrubs" were actually dormant trees, Rinaudo started pruning, tending, and watering them. His work inspired hundreds of thousands of farmers to save their failing farms by restoring nearby forests, reversing soil erosion. Farmers in Niger, for example, have doubled their crops and their income, providing food for an additional 2.5 million people per year.

In John 15, Jesus, the creator of agriculture, referred to similar farming tactics when He said, "I am the true vine, and my Father is the gardener. He cuts off every branch in me that bears no fruit, while every branch that does bear fruit he prunes so that it will be even more fruitful" (vv. 1–2).

Without the daily tending of God, our souls grow barren and dry. When we delight in His law, however, meditating on it day and night, we are "like a tree planted by streams of water" (Psalm 1:3). Our leaves will "not wither" and "whatever [we] do prospers" (v. 3). Pruned and planted in Him, we're evergreen—revived and thriving.

LIFE MOMENT

Do a little research on the ways the people in Niger are reclaiming the land with trees. It will encourage you.

GOD MOMENT

Are there times you feel spiritually dry? Is it possible that you are not taking the nourishment from Jesus that He offers as the true vine?

> When we delight in God's law,
> we are "like a tree planted by
> streams of water" (Psalm 1:3).

65

Enough of Everything

2 Corinthians 9:6-15

God is able to bless you abundantly, so that in all
things . . . you will abound in every good work.

2 Corinthians 9:8

Back in the days of much lower prices, a kindergartner went off to school with a dime in his pocket to buy a carton of milk to go with his lunch. When he went home that afternoon, his mother asked if he had purchased the milk. "No," he replied, bursting into tears. "The milk was five cents and I only had a dime."

How often have we responded to demands placed upon us with the same childish understanding? According to the Bible, we have all the resources we need at our disposal in regard to service for Jesus—yet we're often reluctant to act because we fear we won't have what it takes. But the Bible assures us that God has provided us with every blessing in abundance. By His grace, we have everything we need to do the tasks He has for us (2 Corinthians 9:8).

The apostle Paul was not saying that we have enough grace to do anything we want to do. God does not offer us a blank check. No, Paul was giving us the assurance that we have enough grace to do whatever God has called us to do—whether it is to give money for the cause of the gospel, as the Corinthians were doing (v. 7), or to give love to a difficult teenager, an indifferent spouse, or an aging parent.

Whatever the task, God will make sure we "abound in every good work" (v. 8).

LIFE MOMENT
What is your favorite blessing from God?

GOD MOMENT
What is the "good work" you think God has called you to do for Him?

> *We have enough grace to do*
> *whatever God has called us to do.*

66

The Greatness of Gratitude

Luke 17:11–19

One of them, when he saw that he was healed,
came back, praising God in a loud voice.

Luke 17:15

Jesus was on His way to Jerusalem when ten lepers approached Him. Standing at a distance, as lepers were required to do, they called to Him: "Jesus, Master, have pity on us!" (Luke 17:13).

When Jesus saw them, He commanded, "Go, show yourselves to the priests" (v. 14), for he was the one who could declare them healed and no longer unclean. As they were on their way, the ten lepers were healed.

One of them, when he saw that he was healed, came back, threw himself at Jesus's feet, and thanked Him. "Where are the nine?" Jesus asked.

Good question.

Jesus referred to the grateful man as a Samaritan—an outsider—perhaps to underscore His saying that "the people of this world are more shrewd . . . than are the people of light" (16:8). The word translated *shrewd* has the connotation of "thoughtful" or "wise." Sometimes people of the world have better manners than Jesus's followers do.

In the busyness of life, we may forget to give thanks. Someone has done something for us—given a gift, performed a task, delivered a timely sermon, provided a word of counsel or comfort. But we fail to say thanks.

Has someone done something for you this week? Give that friend a call or text to say thanks. After all, "Love has good manners" (1 Corinthians 13:5 PHILLIPS).

LIFE MOMENT

Are you known to others—wife, friends, coworkers—as being grateful? Think of an example where gratitude encouraged someone else.

GOD MOMENT

The fact that Jesus asked, "Where are the nine?" should make us aware of something vital. God notices our actions (such as whether we are thankful), and He deserves an accounting for them.

> *Sometimes people of the world have better manners than Jesus's followers do.*

67

Tug-of-War

Philippians 2:1–4, 4:1–3

Make my joy complete by being like-minded, having
the same love, being one in spirit and of one mind.

Philippians 2:2

A small college in Michigan has an interesting annual rite—a tug-of-war. Two teams train and prepare to pull together on their end of the rope to win the competition, hoping to avoid the mud-pit between the teams and gain campus bragging rights for another year. For a fun competition, it can become intense.

As believers in Jesus, we often face the challenge of learning how to pull together. Self-interest, personal agendas, and power struggles get in the way of genuine ministry and hinder the work of Christ.

Such was the case in Paul's letter to the Philippians, where he had to plead with Euodia and Syntyche to be of the same mind (4:2). Their personal friction created a roadblock to their spiritual service, and their "tug-of-war" was harming the life of the church.

Paul's appeal was for them to pull together and work for the honor of the Master. It is an appeal that serves us well today. When we feel distanced from our fellow believers, we must look for the common ground we have in the Savior.

Church is no place for a tug-of-war. It's imperative that we work together for the advancement of God's kingdom. He can use us in wonderful ways when we lay aside our personal differences and pull together on the rope.

LIFE MOMENT

Is there a tug-of-war issue going on between you and another believer in Jesus? What can you do to help solve the problem?

GOD MOMENT

Under God's inspiration, Paul said we should be "like-minded . . . of one mind" as believers. Why is this so important?

> *When we feel distanced from fellow believers, we must look for the common ground we have in the Savior.*

68

The Contents of Lincoln's Pockets

Romans 15:1–13

Each of us should please our neighbors
for their good, to build them up.

Romans 15:2

The night US president Abraham Lincoln was shot at Ford's Theater in 1865, his pockets contained the following: two spectacles, a lens polisher, a pocketknife, a watch fob, a handkerchief, a leather wallet containing a five-dollar Confederate bill, and eight newspaper clippings, including several that praised him and his policies.

We may wonder what the Confederate money was doing in the President's pocket, but it's easy to speculate about the glowing news stories. Everyone needs encouragement, even a great leader like Lincoln! Can you see him, in the moments before the fateful play, perhaps reading them to his wife?

Who do you know who needs encouragement? Everyone! Look around you. There isn't one person in your line of vision who is as confident as they seem. We're all one failure, snide comment, or bad hair day away from self-doubt.

What if we all obeyed God's command to "please our neighbors for their good, to build them up"? (Romans 15:2). What if we determined only to speak "gracious words" that are "sweet to the soul and healing to the bones"? (Proverbs 16:24). What if we wrote these words down, so friends could reread and savor them? Then we'd all have notes in our pockets (or on our phones!). And we'd be more like Jesus, who "did not please himself" but lived for others (Romans 15:3).

LIFE MOMENT

If you are married, what would be something you would like to be reading to your wife in the last minutes of your life?

GOD MOMENT

The second great commandment of Jesus in the New Testament is for us to love our neighbors as ourselves. How can you do that today in a real, tangible way—keeping in mind that our neighbors are anyone we encounter throughout the day?

> *Who do you know who needs encouragement? Everyone! Look around you.*

69

A Friend of Sinners

Matthew 9:9-13

I have not come to call the righteous,
but sinners to repentance.

Luke 5:32

Jesus was having dinner one evening when "many tax collectors and sinners came and ate with him" (Matthew 9:10). The religious leaders of that day were outraged by His behavior. Their conclusion was that Jesus was a friend of sinners, and as it turns out, He was. "The Son of Man came to seek and to save the lost" (Luke 19:10).

Jesus was morally separate from sinners and never took part in their lifestyle. Yet He did not separate himself physically from sinful people. He spent time with them and became their friend.

Just like Jesus, you and I can't help but rub shoulders with all kinds of people in our daily activities. Tertullian, an early Roman writer, described the relationships between the Christians and non-Christians of his day this way: "We live among you, eat the same food, wear the same clothes. . . . We sojourn with you in the world, renouncing neither forum, nor market, nor bath, nor booth, nor workshop, nor inn. . . . We till the ground with you, we join with you in business ventures."

We too must seek the lost, as Jesus did—and it doesn't take much effort. It's good to ask ourselves from time to time, "How many friends do I have who don't know Jesus?"

LIFE MOMENT

Who do you know who needs to meet Jesus as Savior? Imagine what it would be like to see him or her trust Jesus.

GOD MOMENT

Of course Jesus felt free to seek the lost; He was God in the flesh. What does the Bible say about why you need to guide people to Jesus?

> *Jesus was morally separate from sinners and never took part in their lifestyle. Yet He did not separate himself physically from sinful people.*

70

Objects in Mirror

Philippians 3:7-14

Forgetting what is behind and straining toward what is ahead, I press on toward the goal to win the prize for which God has called me heavenward in Christ Jesus.

Philippians 3:13-14

M ust. Go. Faster." That's what Dr. Ian Malcolm, played by Jeff Goldblum, says in an iconic scene from the 1993 movie *Jurassic Park* as he and two other characters flee in a Jeep from a rampaging tyrannosaurus. When the driver looks in the rearview mirror, he sees the raging reptile's jaw—right above the words: "OBJECTS IN MIRROR MAY BE CLOSER THAN THEY APPEAR."

The scene is a masterful combination of intensity and grim humor. But sometimes the "monsters" from our past feel like they'll never stop pursuing us. We look in the "mirror" of our lives and see mistakes looming right there, threatening to consume us with guilt or shame.

The apostle Paul understood the past's potentially paralyzing power. He'd spent years trying to live perfectly apart from Christ, and he even persecuted Christians (Philippians 3:1–9). Regret over his past could easily have crippled him.

But Paul found such beauty and power in his relationship with Christ that he was compelled to let go of his old life (vv. 8–9). That freed him to look forward in faith instead of backward in fear or regret: "One thing

I do: Forgetting what is behind and straining toward what is ahead, I press on toward the goal" (vv. 13–14).

Our redemption in Christ has freed us to live for Him. We don't have to let those "objects in (our) mirror" dictate our direction as we continue forward.

LIFE MOMENT

Everybody who has ever driven has a "rearview mirror" story. What's one you tell others about?

GOD MOMENT

Is there something "pursuing" you that you need to let go of and turn over to the Lord?

> *Paul found such beauty and power in his relationship with Christ that he was compelled to let go of his old life.*

71

Unbreakable in Jesus

Jeremiah 1:4-10

"Do not be afraid of them, for I am with you
and will rescue you," declares the LORD.

Jeremiah 1:8

Louis Zamperini's military plane crashed at sea during World War II, killing eight of eleven men onboard. "Louie" and two others clambered into life rafts. They drifted for forty-seven days, fending off sharks, riding out storms, ducking bullets from an enemy plane, and catching and eating raw fish and birds. They finally drifted onto an island and were immediately captured. For two years Louie was beaten, tortured, and worked mercilessly as a prisoner of war. His remarkable story is told in the book *Unbroken* by Laura Hillenbrand.

Jeremiah is one of the Bible's unbreakable characters. He endured enemy plots (Jeremiah 11:18), was whipped and put in stocks (20:2), flogged and bound in a dungeon (37:15–16), and lowered by ropes into the deep mire of a cistern (38:6). He survived because God had promised to stay with him and rescue him (1:8). God makes a similar promise to us: "Never will I leave you; never will I forsake you" (Hebrews 13:5). God didn't promise to save Jeremiah or us from trouble, but He has promised to carry us through trouble.

Louie recognized God's protection, and after the war he gave his life to Jesus. He forgave his captors and led some to Christ. Louie realized that while we can't avoid all problems, we need not suffer them alone. When we face them with Jesus, we become unbreakable.

LIFE MOMENT

The heroism of people like Louis Zamperini is admirable. Who do you consider a hero in today's world?

GOD MOMENT

What struggles are you facing? Have you turned them over to Jesus—accepting His help and guidance?

> God didn't promise to save Jeremiah or us from trouble, but He has promised to carry us through trouble.

72

"The Lord's"

Isaiah 44:1-5

The Spirit himself testifies with our spirit
that we are God's children.

Romans 8:16

I t doesn't take much to notice that getting "inked" is very popular these days. Some tattoos are so small that one barely notices them. Some people—from athletes to actors to everyday people—have opted to cover much of their bodies with multicolored inks, words, and designs. The trend seems like it's here to stay, a trend that netted $3 billion in revenue in a recent year—and an additional $66 million for tattoo removal.

Regardless of how you may feel about tattoos, Isaiah 44 speaks metaphorically about people writing something on their hands: "The Lord's" (v. 5). This "self-tattoo" is the climax of an entire paragraph that speaks of the Lord's care for those He had chosen (v. 1). They could count on His help (v. 2), and their land and descendants were marked for blessing (v. 3). Two simple, powerful words, "The Lord's," affirmed that God's people knew they were His possession and that He would take care of them.

Those who come to God through faith in Jesus Christ can confidently say of themselves, "The Lord's!" We are His people, His sheep, His offspring, His inheritance, His dwelling. These are the things we cling to in the varied seasons of life. While we may have no external mark or tattoo identifying us as God's, we have the witness of God's Spirit in our hearts that we belong to Him (see Romans 8:16–17).

LIFE MOMENT

If you were to get a tattoo that had just one word, what word would you pick?

GOD MOMENT

In the author's list of advantages of being the Lord's, he mentions being His sheep, His offspring, His inheritance, and His dwelling. Which of these has the most meaning for you?

> *Those who come to God through faith in Jesus Christ are His people, His sheep, His offspring, His inheritance, His dwelling.*

73
Eating Words
Ezekiel 2:7–3:4

Son of man, eat what is before you, eat this scroll;
then go and speak to the people of Israel.
Ezekiel 3:1

An Australian woman developed a craving for paper. She began her unusual diet as a child, and as she grew older she ate as many as ten tissues and a half page of the newspaper every day. The woman had also consumed small quantities of blotting paper, sheets from exercise books, and petty cash vouchers.

That woman's strange habit may sound a little like what the prophet was talking about in Ezekiel 3, but his "eating" is to be taken as symbolic. Ezekiel was illustrating a spiritual exercise that all of us should engage in. If we are to declare God's truth with meaning and power, we must take time to let it fill our hearts. We need to feel the implications of what God has said. We are to let His Word become a vital part of us so we can't talk about it glibly as uninvolved, detached students, but as those who have personally "tasted" it.

The actual words and thoughts of God are revealed in the Bible. Don't just read them and repeat them. Think them. Feel them. Ask the Lord to clarify them—to make them a part of your experience and to teach you.

Yes, today's Bible reading contains a profound principle: We must "eat" the Word before we speak it. Maybe then we won't have to eat our own words later on.

LIFE MOMENT

What are your favorite sections of the Bible? Psalms? Epistles? Gospels? Something else?

GOD MOMENT

Pause and think about the sentence below. How does that push your desire to dive a little deeper into God's Word?

> *The actual words and thoughts of God are revealed in the Bible.*

74

Listening Matters

Psalm 85

I will listen to what God the LORD says.

Psalm 85:8

"C ome at once. We have struck a berg." Those were the first words Harold Cottam, the wireless operator on the RMS *Carpathia*, received from the sinking RMS *Titanic* at 12:25 a.m. on April 15, 1912. The *Carpathia* would be the first ship to the disaster scene, saving 706 lives.

In the US Senate hearings days later, the *Carpathia*'s captain Arthur Rostron testified, "The whole thing was absolutely providential. . . . The wireless operator was in his cabin at the time, not on official business at all, but just simply listening as he was undressing. . . . In ten minutes maybe he would have been in bed, and we would not have heard the message."

Listening matters—especially listening to God. The writers of Psalm 85, the sons of Korah, urged attentive obedience when they wrote, "I will listen to what God the LORD says; he promises peace to his people, his faithful servants—but let them not turn to folly. Surely his salvation is near those who fear him" (vv. 8–9). Their admonition is especially poignant because their ancestor Korah had rebelled against God and had perished in the wilderness (Numbers 16:1–35).

The night the *Titanic* sank, another ship was much closer, but its wireless operator had gone to bed. Had he heard the distress signal, perhaps more lives would have been saved. When we listen to God by obeying His teaching, He'll help us navigate life's most troubled waters.

LIFE MOMENT

When has not listening well gotten you into a bit of trouble?

GOD MOMENT

What are some spiritual activities that help you "hear" from God?

> *Listening matters—especially listening to God.*

75

No Longer Afraid

Zephaniah 3:9-17

They will eat and lie down and no one will make them afraid.

Zephaniah 3:13

When the Ethiopian police found her a week after her abduction, three black-maned lions surrounded her, guarding her as though she were their own. Seven men had kidnapped the twelve-year-old girl, carried her into the woods and beaten her. Miraculously, however, a small pride of lions heard the girl's cries, came running, and chased off the attackers. "[The lions] stood guard until we found her and then they just left her like a gift and went back into the forest," police Sergeant Wondimu Wedajo told one reporter.

There are days when violence and evil, like that inflicted on this young girl, overpower us, leaving us without hope and terrified. In ancient times, the people of Judah experienced this. They were overrun by ferocious armies and unable to imagine any possibility of escape. Fear consumed them. However, God always renewed His unrelenting presence with His people: "The LORD, the King of Israel, is with you; never again will you fear any harm" (Zephaniah 3:15). Even when our catastrophes result from our own rebellion, God still comes to our rescue. "The LORD your God is with you," we hear, "the Mighty Warrior who saves" (v. 17).

Whatever troubles overtake us, whatever evils, Jesus—the Lion of Judah—is with us (Revelation 5:5). No matter how alone we feel, our strong Savior is with us. No matter what fears ravage us, our God assures us that He is by our side.

LIFE MOMENT

What is the greatest rescue story you've experienced in life? Have you ever been lost? Stranded? In the wrong place at the wrong time?

GOD MOMENT

When have you felt God's presence in the middle of a difficult situation—where He was your only resource?

> *Even when our catastrophes result from our own rebellion, God still comes to our rescue.*

76

Moving Toward Spiritual Maturity

Ephesians 4:11-16

Become mature, attaining to the whole
measure of the fullness of Christ.

Ephesians 4:13

A recent survey asked respondents to identify the age at which they believed they became adults. Those who considered themselves adults pointed to specific behaviors as evidence of their status. Having a budget and buying a house topped the list as being marks of "adulting." Other adult activities ranged from cooking dinner every weeknight and scheduling one's own medical appointments, to the more humorous ability to choose to eat snacks for dinner or being excited to stay at home on a Saturday evening instead of going out.

The Bible says we should press on toward spiritual maturity as well. Paul wrote to the church at Ephesus, urging the people to "become mature, attaining to the whole measure of the fullness of Christ" (Ephesians 4:13). While we're "young" in our faith, we're vulnerable to "every wind of teaching" (v. 14), which often results in division among us. Instead, as we mature in our understanding of the truth, we function as a unified body under "him who is the head, that is, Christ" (v. 15).

God gave us His Spirit to help us grow into a full understanding of who He is (John 14:26), and He equips pastors and teachers to instruct and lead us toward maturity in our faith (Ephesians 4:11–12). Just as certain characteristics are evidence of physical maturity, our unity as His body is evidence of our spiritual growth.

LIFE MOMENT

What do you think of this idea of calling what grown-ups do "adulting"? When did you consider yourself a full adult?

GOD MOMENT

Where do you think you are on the scale of spiritual maturity? If you are not satisfied that you are as mature as you should be in your relationship with the Lord, what changes can you make?

> *God gave us His Spirit to help us grow into a full understanding of who He is.*

77

No Rushing Prayer

Psalm 46

Be still, and know that I am God.

Psalm 46:10

Alice Kaholusuna recounts a story of how the Hawaiian people would sit outside their temples for a lengthy amount of time preparing themselves before entering in. Even after entering, they would creep to the altar to offer their prayers. Afterward, they would sit outside again for a long time to "breathe life" into their prayers. When missionaries came to the island, the Hawaiians sometimes considered their prayers odd. The missionaries would stand up, utter a few sentences, call them "prayer," say amen, and be done with it. The Hawaiians described these prayers as "without breath."

Alice's story speaks of how God's people may not always take the opportunity to "be still, and know" (Psalm 46:10). Make no mistake—God hears our prayers, whether they're quick or slow. But often the pace of our lives mimics the pace of our hearts, and we need to allow ample time for God to speak into not only our lives but also the lives of those around us. How many life-giving moments have we missed by rushing, saying amen, and being done with it?

We're often impatient with everything from slow people to the slow lane in traffic. Yet, I believe God in His kindness says, "Be still. Breathe in and out. Go slow, and remember that I am God, your refuge and strength, an ever-present help in trouble." To do so is to know that God is God. To do so is to trust. To do so is to live.

LIFE MOMENT

Would you call yourself patient or impatient in regard to traffic, lines at the grocery story, and waiting for things to download?

GOD MOMENT

What would be the advantage of being still, being patient, and waiting for God when it comes time for devotions for yourself or with the family?

> *Perhaps God would say, "Be still. Go slow. Remember that I am God, your refuge and strength."*

78

Read a Banned Book

Jeremiah 36:1-8, 21-26

Write . . . all the words that I have spoken to
you . . . that everyone may turn from his evil way,
that I may forgive their iniquity and their sin.

Jeremiah 36:2-3 NKJV

Each year the American Library Association designates a Banned
Books Week in celebration of the freedom to read and to express
one's opinion "even if that opinion might be considered unorthodox
or unpopular."

The Bible is the all-time bestselling book, but in some parts of the
world it is banned because it's considered dangerous. The Bible is dangerous, however, only to those who fear finding out that they are wrong.
It's dangerous to those who exploit the weak and the innocent, who use
force to keep others enslaved in poverty and ignorance, who don't want
to give up their favorite sin, who believe that salvation can be found
apart from Christ.

No one wants to be told they are wrong. No one wants to hear that
their behavior is putting themselves and those they love in danger or
that God's patience will eventually wear out. Yet that was the message
God told Jeremiah to write (Jeremiah 36:2). When His message was
read to King Jehoiakim, the king cut up the scroll and threw it into the
fire (v. 23).

The only way to know we are right is to be willing to discover where we are wrong. Read the all-time bestselling banned book, and let it reveal to you the truth about God—and about yourself.

LIFE MOMENT

What do you think would be a good reason to ban a book? Or do you think no books should be banned?

GOD MOMENT

Other than salvation—the most important truth—what are a couple of biblical truths that you think are essential?

> *The Bible is dangerous only to those who fear finding out that they are wrong.*

79

Something to Say

Isaiah 50:4-10

The Sovereign LORD has given me a well-instructed
tongue, to know the word that sustains the weary.

Isaiah 50:4

According to *Einstein Recollections*, a document compiled by Peter Van De Kamp, Albert Einstein was asked to speak at Swarthmore College in Pennsylvania. He replied to the invitation with this, "Thank you very much, but I have nothing to say."

Later, he sent a message to the president of the college: "Now I have something to say, may I come?" President Frank Aydelotte responded by asking Einstein to deliver the commencement address for the Class of 1938, which he did on June 6 that year.

Perhaps you have had opportunities "to speak a word in season" to those who are weary (Isaiah 50:4 NKJV), but you didn't feel as if you had anything to say. If so, follow the example of the Servant of the Lord, the promised Messiah, whom we read about in Isaiah 50:4–10. Because He listened and obeyed what He heard, He had a message to give to others.

Open God's Word with an eagerness to learn and do what He tells you to do. Think of the Lord as present and speaking to you, disclosing His mind and emotions and will.

Meditate on His words till you know what He is saying.

Then, as the Servant discovered, in time God will give you "a well-instructed tongue" (v. 4). If you listen to the Lord, you'll have something worth saying.

LIFE MOMENT

When the opportunity to speak out comes up, how do you usually respond?

GOD MOMENT

The key part of Isaiah 50:4 is this, "the Lord God has given me the tongue of the learned" (NKJV). While these words refer specifically to Jesus, we can be thankful for God's provision of speech to us that allows us to share truth with others.

> *Open God's Word with an eagerness to learn and do what He tells you to do.*

80

Tears in Heaven

Revelation 21:1-8

> [God] will wipe every tear from their eyes. There will
> be no more death or mourning or crying or pain.
>
> Revelation 21:4

In 1991, famed British guitarist Eric Clapton was stricken with grief when his four-year-old son Conor died as a result of a fall from an apartment window. Looking for an outlet for his grief, Clapton penned perhaps his most poignant ballad: "Tears in Heaven." It seems that every note weighs heavy with the sense of pain and loss that can be understood only by a parent who has lost a child.

Surprisingly, however, Clapton said in a television interview years later, "In a sense, it wasn't even a sad song. It was a song of belief. When it [says that] there will be no more tears in heaven, I think it's a song of optimism—of reunion."

The thought of a heavenly reunion is powerful indeed. For everyone who has trusted Jesus Christ for salvation, there is the hope that we will be reunited forever in a place where God "will wipe every tear from [our] eyes. There will be no more death or mourning or crying or pain" (Revelation 21:4). And, most of all, it is a place where we will "see his face" and forever be with Christ himself (22:4).

In our times of loss and grief, of tears and sorrow, isn't it comforting to know that Christ has purchased for us a heavenly home where there will be no more tears!

LIFE MOMENT

Who are you looking forward to being reunited with in heaven? How does Revelation 21:4 help you as you look ahead?

GOD MOMENT

Turn the tables on our usual view of arriving in heaven. How will Jesus respond when He sees you? How amazing will that be?

> *The thought of a heavenly reunion is powerful indeed.*

81

No More Running

Jonah 1:1–10

In my distress I called to the LORD, and he answered
me. From deep in the realm of the dead I called
for help, and you listened to my cry.

Jonah 2:2

On July 18, 1983, a US Air Force captain disappeared from Albuquerque, New Mexico, without a trace. Thirty-five years later, authorities found him in California. The *New York Times* reported that, "depressed about his job," he had simply run away.

Thirty-five years on the run! Half a lifetime spent looking over his shoulder! I have to imagine that anxiety and paranoia were this man's constant companions.

But I have to admit, I also know a bit about being "on the run." No, I've never abruptly fled something in my life . . . physically. But at times I know there's something God wants me to do, something I need to face or confess. I don't want to do it. And so, in my own way, I run too.

The prophet Jonah is infamous for literally running from God's assignment to preach to the city of Nineveh (see Jonah 1:1–3). But he couldn't outrun God. You've probably heard what happened (vv. 4, 17): A storm. A fish. A swallowing. And in the belly of the beast, a reckoning, in which Jonah faced what he'd done and cried to God for help (2:2)

Jonah wasn't a perfect prophet. But I take comfort in his remarkable story, because, even despite Jonah's stubbornness, God never let go of him. The Lord still answered the man's desperate prayer, graciously restoring His reluctant servant (v. 2)—just as He does with us.

LIFE MOMENT

We've all had those "gotta get away" moments. Can you recall a time when you felt the best thing would be to run from your situation?

GOD MOMENT

In a "fight or flight" moment, what does God offer you to help you stick around and find a solution to the difficulty you're in?

> *Despite Jonah's stubbornness,*
> *God never let go of him.*

82

Facing the Battles with God

Psalm 11

In the LORD I take refuge.

Psalm 11:1

The heroic deeds of US Army soldier Desmond Doss are featured in the movie *Hacksaw Ridge*. While Doss's convictions wouldn't allow him to take human life, as an army medic he committed himself to preserving life even at the risk of his own. The citation read at Doss's Medal of Honor ceremony on October 12, 1945, included these words: "Private First Class Doss refused to seek cover and remained in the fire-swept area with the many stricken, carrying them one by one to the edge of the escarpment. . . . He unhesitatingly braved enemy shelling and small arms fire to assist an artillery officer."

In Psalm 11, David's conviction that his refuge was in God compelled him to resist suggestions to flee rather than face his foes (vv. 2–3). Six simple words comprised his statement of faith: "In the LORD I take refuge" (v. 1). That well-rooted conviction would guide his conduct.

David's words in verses 4–7 amplified God's greatness. Yes, life can sometimes be like a battlefield, and hostile fire can send us scattering for cover when we're bombarded with health challenges or financial, relational, and spiritual stresses. So, what should we do? Acknowledge that

God is the king of the universe (v. 4); take delight in His amazing capacity to judge with precision (vv. 5–6); and rest in His delight in what's right, fair, and equitable (v. 7). We can run swiftly to God for shelter!

LIFE MOMENT

If you served in the military or had a family member who did, what was the most frightening event you or a military family member experienced?

GOD MOMENT

In which of life's frightening moments do you most readily seek God's shelter? How does He help?

> *Six simple words comprised David's statement of faith: "In the LORD I take refuge."*

83

Humble Love

Philippians 2:1-11

The greatest among you will be your servant.
Matthew 23:11

When Benjamin Franklin was a young man, he made a list of twelve virtues he desired to grow in over the course of his life. He showed it to a friend, who suggested he add "humility" to it. Franklin liked the idea. He then added some guidelines to help him with each item on the list. Among Franklin's thoughts about humility, he held up Jesus as an example to emulate.

Jesus shows us the ultimate example of humility. God's Word tells us, "In your relationships with one another, have the same mindset as Christ Jesus: Who, being in very nature God, did not consider equality with God something to be used to his own advantage; rather, he made himself nothing by taking the very nature of a servant" (Philippians 2:5–7).

Jesus demonstrated the greatest humility of all. Though eternally with the Father, He chose to bend beneath a cross in love so that through His death He might lift any who receive Him into the joy of His presence.

We imitate Jesus's humility when we seek to serve our heavenly Father by serving others. Jesus's kindness helps us catch a breathtaking glimpse of the beauty of setting ourselves aside to attend to others' needs. Aiming for humility isn't easy in our "me first" world. But as we rest securely in our Savior's love, He will give us everything we need to follow Him.

LIFE MOMENT

Who do you know who is a great example of humility—an accomplished person who takes little credit for what he or she has been able to do?

GOD MOMENT

Are there any areas of life where you need to increase the humility and take a bit of a break from the pride—realizing that all you can do comes from God anyway?

> *We imitate Jesus's humility when we seek to serve our heavenly Father by serving others.*

84

Campaign of Reconciliation

Luke 19:1–10

The Son of Man came to seek and to save the lost.

Luke 19:10

I n Craig Nelson's book *The First Heroes*, we read about the Doolittle Raiders, who launched the first major counterattack on the Pacific front during World War II. Not all of the "raiders" returned from their bombing mission. Jacob DeShazer was among those who were captured and held in prisoner of war camps under difficult and painful circumstances.

DeShazer later returned to Japan after the war, but not to seek revenge. He had received Jesus as his Savior and had come back to Japanese soil carrying the message of Christ. A former warrior who was once on a campaign of war was now on a campaign of reconciliation.

DeShazer's mission to Japan mirrors the heart of the Savior, who himself came on a mission of love and reconciliation. Luke reminds us that when Christ came into the world, it was not merely to be a moral example or a compelling teacher. He came "to seek and to save the lost" (19:10). His love for us found its expression in the cross, and His rescue of us found its realization when He emerged triumphantly from the tomb in resurrected life.

In Christ we find forgiveness, and that forgiveness changes our life and our eternity—all because Jesus came on a campaign of reconciliation.

LIFE MOMENT

What touches you most about your reconciliation with God? What are you most grateful that He has forgiven you for?

GOD MOMENT

The greatness of Jesus's act was that it brought us into a relationship with God we could never earn by ourselves.

> *Christ came into the world not merely to be a moral example or a compelling teacher but "to seek and to save" the lost.*

85

The Discus Thrower

1 Peter 5:6-10

The God of all grace, . . . after you have suffered
a little while, will himself restore you and
make you strong, firm and steadfast.

1 Peter 5:10

A Scottish athlete in the nineteenth century made an iron discus based on a description he read in a book. What he didn't know was that the discus used in official competition was made of wood with only an outer rim of iron. His was solid metal and weighed three or four times as much as those being used by other discus throwers.

According to author John Eldredge, the man marked out the record distance in a field near his home and trained day and night to match it. For years he labored until he could break the record. Then he took his iron discus to England for his first competition.

When he arrived at the games, he was handed the official discus. He easily set a new record, a distance far beyond those of his competitors. He remained the uncontested champion for many years. This man trained under a heavy burden and became better for it.

When we are given a heavy burden to bear in life, we need to learn to bear it in Jesus's strength and for His sake. Whatever the burden or suffering, God can use it to "make you strong, firm and steadfast," as 1 Peter 5:10 says.

Our burdens can make us better than we ever imagined—stronger, more patient, more courageous, more gentle, and more loving than we could otherwise be.

LIFE MOMENT

A men's discus weighs about four and a half pounds. The world record is a toss of 243 1/2 feet. How far do you think you could throw the discus?

GOD MOMENT

What heavy burden are you bearing right now? What is one possible lesson God wants you to learn from it?

> *Our burdens can make us better than we ever imagined.*

86

Unfrozen

Galatians 2:11–16

When Cephas came to Antioch, I opposed him to his face.

Galatians 2:11

At a roundtable discussion about reconciliation, one participant wisely said, "Don't freeze people in time." He observed that we tend to remember mistakes people make and never grant them the opportunity to change.

There are so many moments in Peter's life when God could have "frozen" him in time. But He never did. Peter—the impulsive disciple—"corrected" Jesus, earning a sharp rebuke from the Lord (Matthew 16:21–23). He famously denied Christ (John 18:15–27), only to be restored later (21:15–19). And he once contributed to racial divisions within the church.

The issue arose when Peter (also called Cephas) had separated himself from the Gentiles (Galatians 2:11–12). Only recently he associated freely with them. But some Jews arrived who insisted that circumcision was required for believers in Christ, so Peter began avoiding the uncircumcised Gentiles. This marked a dangerous return to the law of Moses. Paul called Peter's behavior "hypocrisy" (v. 13).

Because of Paul's bold confrontation, the issue was resolved. Peter went on to serve God in the beautiful spirit of unity He intends for us.

No one needs to remain frozen in their worst moments. In God's grace we can embrace each other, learn from each other, confront each other when it's necessary, and grow together in His love.

LIFE MOMENT

Do you know anyone who is still "frozen in time" because of his or her worst moment? How can you and others begin to let it go and let the person move ahead?

GOD MOMENT

How has God's grace and mercy helped you to move on from a bad life incident and helped you get past that moment?

> *No one needs to remain frozen in their worst moments.*

87

Keeping Busy?

Matthew 11:25-30

Come to me, all you who are weary and
burdened, and I will give you rest.
Matthew 11:28

People who are trying to be friendly sometimes ask, "Are you keeping busy?" The question seems harmless, but it carries a subtle message. Beneath the surface is a test of personal value. If we can't rattle off a list of things we have to do, we feel as if we're admitting that we're not worth much.

But does God determine our value by how busy we are? Does He calculate our worth by how much we accomplish? Does He reward us for living on the edge of exhaustion and not taking care of ourselves?

One of the first verses I learned as a child was Matthew 11:28, "Come to me, all you who are weary and burdened, and I will give you rest." It didn't mean much to me at the time because I didn't understand weariness. But now that I'm older, I feel the temptation to keep pace with the world so I won't be left behind.

But followers of Jesus don't have to live like that. Not only has He released us from slavery to sin but also from the bondage of having to prove our worth.

Accomplishing a lot for God may make us feel important, but what makes us important to God is what we allow Him to accomplish in us—conforming us into the image of His Son (Romans 8:28–30).

LIFE MOMENT

How do you feel when you are not busy? Why do people see it as a badge of honor when their lives are overly busy?

GOD MOMENT

Memorize Matthew 11:28, and the next time you feel overwhelmed, let God know that you are asking for the rest He offers.

> *Not only has the Lord released us from slavery to sin but also from the bondage of having to prove our worth.*

88

Escape or Peace?

John 16:25–33

I have told you these things, so that in me you may
have peace. In this world you will have trouble.
But take heart! I have overcome the world.

John 16:33

"Escape." The billboard shouts the benefits of having a hot tub installed. It gets my attention—and gets me thinking. My wife and I have talked about getting a hot tub . . . someday. It'd be like a vacation in our back yard! Except for the cleaning. And the electric bill. And . . . suddenly, the hoped-for escape starts to sound like something I might need escape *from*.

Still, that word entices so effectively because it promises something we want: Relief. Comfort. Security. *Escape.* It's something our culture tempts and teases us with in many ways. Now, there's nothing wrong with resting or a getaway to someplace beautiful. But there's a difference between *escaping* life's hardship and *trusting God* with them.

In John 16, Jesus tells His disciples that the next chapter of their lives will test their faith. "In this world you will have trouble," He summarizes at the end. And then He adds this promise, "But take heart! I have overcome the world" (v. 33). Jesus didn't want His disciples to cave in to despair. Instead, He invited them to trust Him, to know the rest He provides: "I have told you these things," He said, "so that in me you may have peace" (v. 33).

Jesus didn't promise us a pain-free life. But he *does* promise that as we trust and rest in Him, we can experience a peace that's deeper and more satisfying than any escape the world tries to sell us.

LIFE MOMENT

What invitations to escape have you seen in the world around you lately? What makes them appealing?

GOD MOMENT

How do you tell the difference between a valid need for rest and the temptation to escape your troubles? Ask God to help you find the peace and comfort you need in ways that honor Him.

> *There's a difference between escaping life's hardships and trusting God with them.*

89

Full Attention

1 Thessalonians 5:12-18

Rejoice always, pray continually, give
thanks in all circumstances.

1 Thessalonians 5:16-18

Technology today seems to demand our constant attention. The modern "miracle" of the internet gives us the amazing capacity to access humanity's collective learning in the palm of our hand. But for many, such constant access can come at a cost.

Writer Linda Stone has coined the phrase "continual partial attention" to describe the modern impulse to always need to know what's happening "out there," to make sure we're not missing anything. If that sounds like it could produce chronic anxiety, you're right!

Although the apostle Paul struggled with different reasons for anxiety, he knew our souls are wired to find peace in God. Which is why, in a letter to new believers who had endured persecution (1 Thessalonians 2:14), Paul concluded by urging the believers to "rejoice always, pray continually, give thanks in all circumstances" (5:16–18).

Praying "continually" might seem pretty daunting. But then, how often do we check our phones? What if we instead let that urge be a prompt to talk to God? To say thank you, lift up a prayer request, or praise Him?

More important, what if we learned to exchange a need to always be in "the know" for continual, prayerful rest in God's presence? Through relying on Christ's Spirit, we can learn to give our heavenly Father our continual full attention as we make our way through each day.

LIFE MOMENT

In what ways would life change for you if the internet went away?

GOD MOMENT

It seems nearly impossible to pray continually, so what small steps could you take to pray more often?

> *What if we learned to exchange a need to always be in the know for continual, prayerful rest in God's presence?*

90

Ears Were Made for Listening

Jeremiah 5:18-23

Hear this, you foolish and senseless people, who have
eyes but do not see, who have ears but do not hear.

Jeremiah 5:21

ctress Diane Kruger was offered a role that would make her a house-
hold name. But it required her to play a young wife and mother
experiencing the loss of her husband and child, and she had never
personally suffered loss to such a degree. She didn't know if she could be
believable. But she accepted, and in order to prepare, she began attending
support meetings for people walking through the valley of extreme grief.

Initially she offered suggestions and thoughts when those in the
group shared their stories. She, like most of us, wanted to be helpful.
But gradually she stopped talking, and simply started listening. It was
only then she began truly learning to walk a mile in their shoes. And her
realization came by using her ears.

Jeremiah's indictment against the people was that they refused to use
their "ears" to hear the Lord's voice. The prophet did not mince words,
calling them "foolish and senseless people" (Jeremiah 5:21). God is con-
stantly at work in our lives communicating words of love, instruction,
encouragement, and caution. The Father's desire is that you and I learn

and mature, and we have each been given the tools, such as ears, to do so. The question then is, will we use them to hear the heart of our Father?

LIFE MOMENT

Do you find it difficult to listen instead of talking sometimes? Would your friends call you a talker or a listener?

GOD MOMENT

One of the toughest questions we can answer as Christians is this: How can we listen to God? What are things you can do to help hear from Him?

> God is constantly at work in our lives communicating words of love, instruction, encouragement, and caution.

91

Bowling a Googly

1 Peter 4:12-19

Do not be surprised at the fiery ordeal that has
come to test you, . . . But rejoice inasmuch as
you participate in the sufferings of Christ.

1 Peter 4:12-13

George Bernard Shaw once said, "England and America are two countries separated by a common language." An example from the world of sports demonstrates his point.

As a lifelong baseball fan, I'm familiar with the term *curveball*. It's a ball thrown by the pitcher in such a way that it changes direction, fooling the batter. In cricket, the strategy is similar but the word is very different. The bowler (pitcher) tries to overcome the batsman by "bowling a googly" (pitching a curveball).

Though games and cultures differ, the concept of the curveball portrays a reality familiar in any language. Life is full of times when we are unsuspectingly "bowled a googly," and we find ourselves overwhelmed. In those moments of fear and confusion, it's comforting to know we have a God who is sufficient for any challenge.

Trials are to be expected (1 Peter 4:12). Yet we may well be shocked by the circumstances facing us. But God is never surprised! He permits our trials, and He can enable us to respond to them in a way that honors Him.

When we suffer, we must "continue to do good," wrote Peter (v. 19). In God's strength, we can face life's most troublesome curveballs.

LIFE MOMENT

Which do you think would be harder to hit—a curve thrown by a baseball pitcher or a googly tossed by a cricket bowler?

GOD MOMENT

What good does it do for us to stand in there against the "curveballs" life throws at us? What is the alternative to facing our trials?

> *It's comforting to know we have a God who is sufficient for any challenge.*

92

Flying Machines

Psalm 6

I am worn out from my groaning. All night long I flood
my bed with weeping and drench my couch with tears.

Psalm 6:6

Recording artist James Taylor exploded onto the music scene in early 1970 with the song "Fire and Rain." In it, he talked about the disappointments of life, describing them as "sweet dreams and flying machines in pieces on the ground." That was a reference to Taylor's original band Flying Machine, whose attempt at breaking into the recording industry had failed badly, causing him to wonder if his dreams of a musical career would ever come true. The reality of crushed expectations had taken their toll, leaving Taylor with a sense of loss and hopelessness.

The psalmist David also experienced hopeless despair as he struggled with his own failures, the attacks of others, and the disappointments of life. In Psalm 6:6 he said, "I am worn out from my groaning. All night long I flood my bed with weeping and drench my couch with tears." The depth of his sorrow and loss drove him to heartache—but in that grief he turned to the God of all comfort. David's own crushed and broken "flying machines" gave way to the assurance of God's care, prompting him to say, "The LORD has heard my cry for mercy; the LORD accepts my prayer" (v. 9).

In our own seasons of disappointment, we too can find comfort in God, who cares for our broken hearts.

LIFE MOMENT
What "flying machines" have crashed to the ground around your life?

GOD MOMENT
How have you experienced God's care when you needed His comfort?

> In David's grief, he turned to the God of all comfort.

93

Never Enough

Ecclesiastes 1:1-11

The eye never has enough of seeing.
Ecclesiastes 1:8

In 1968 Frank Borman commanded Apollo 8, the first space mission to circle the moon. He wasn't impressed. The trip took two days both ways. Frank got motion sickness and threw up. He said being weightless was cool—for thirty seconds. Then he got used to it. Up close he found the moon drab and pockmarked with craters. His crew took pictures of the gray wasteland, then became bored.

Frank went where no one had gone before. It wasn't enough. If he quickly tired of an experience that was out of this world, perhaps we should lower our expectations for what lies in this one. The teacher of Ecclesiastes observed that no earthly experience delivers ultimate joy. "The eye never has enough of seeing, nor the ear its fill of hearing" (1:8). We may feel moments of ecstasy, but our elation soon wears off and we seek the next thrill.

Frank had one exhilarating moment, when he saw the earth rise from the darkness behind the moon. Like a blue and white swirled marble, our world sparkled in the sun's light. Similarly, our truest joy comes from the Son shining on us. Jesus is our life, the only ultimate source of meaning, love, and beauty. Our deepest satisfaction comes from out of this world. Our problem? We can go all the way to the moon, yet still not go far enough.

LIFE MOMENT

Have you ever gone somewhere that everyone else thought was absolutely amazing—but found yourself less than impressed? Why was that?

GOD MOMENT

What excites you most about your relationship with God? How does knowing Jesus as Savior give you a perspective that is satisfying?

> The teacher of Ecclesiastes observed that no earthly experience delivers ultimate joy.

94

Death Zone

2 Samuel 11:1-6, 12-15

But David remained in Jerusalem.

2 Samuel 11:1

In 2019, a climber saw his last sunrise from the peak of Mount Everest. He survived the dangerous ascent, but the high altitude squeezed his heart, and he passed away on the trek down. One medical expert warns climbers not to think of the summit as their journey's end. They must get up and down quickly, remembering "they're in the death zone."

David survived his dangerous climb to the top. He killed lions and bears, slew Goliath, dodged Saul's spear and pursuing army, and conquered Philistines and Ammonites to become king of the mountain.

But David forgot he was in the death zone. At the peak of his success, as "the LORD gave David victory wherever he went" (2 Samuel 8:6), he committed adultery and murder. His initial mistake? He lingered on the mountaintop. When his army set out for new challenges, he "remained in Jerusalem" (11:1). David once had volunteered to fight Goliath; now he relaxed in the accolades of his triumphs.

It's hard to stay grounded when everyone, including God, says you're special (7:11–16). But we must. If we've achieved some success, we may appropriately celebrate the accomplishment and accept congratulations, but we must keep moving. We're in the death zone. Come down the mountain. Humbly serve others in the valley—asking God to guard your heart and your steps.

LIFE MOMENT

What do you feel was the greatest accomplishment of your life? How did that change who you are?

GOD MOMENT

The apostle Paul said that we are to forget the things behind us and move on ahead (Philippians 3:13)—and that includes even in good things. What keeps you going for God when you'd rather sit back and bask in something good you've done?

> *It's hard to stay grounded when everyone, including God, says you're special.*

95

Tensile Strength

2 Corinthians 12:7-10

My grace is sufficient for you, for my power
is made perfect in weakness.

2 Corinthians 12:9

When a new highway was being completed in West Michigan, a real danger was discovered. The bridges had been designed to bear their own weight—but not the traffic they were intended to carry. Before the highway could be opened, several bridges had to be re-engineered and rebuilt.

Engineers have to be especially concerned with the tensile strength of the material in their construction plans for structures that are required to bear large amounts of stress due to weight. Tensile strength is the maximum amount of stretching a material can withstand before it tears. If the engineer miscalculates, the structure may collapse under the pressure.

When we are under the weight of stress and hardship, we may wonder whether our Lord, who engineered us, has miscalculated our personal "tensile strength." We are certain that we are going to collapse under the weight of the trials, but our Designer knows exactly what we can handle by His grace. He knows our limits and will never permit more than we can bear. As Bible teacher Ron Hutchcraft said, "God may send a load, but He never sends an overload!"

Reinforced by the steel of God's provision, our tensile strength won't fail.

LIFE MOMENT

Right now, what situation is testing your strength?

GOD MOMENT

Our heavenly Father offers sufficient grace and perfect strength according to 2 Corinthians 12:9. What, exactly, does that mean when you are struggling?

> *Our Designer knows exactly what we can handle by His grace.*

96

Facing the Darkness

Isaiah 9:2-6

The people walking in darkness have seen a great light.

Isaiah 9:2

In the mid-1960s, two people participated in research on the effects of darkness on the human psyche. They entered separate caves, while researchers tracked their eating and sleeping habits. One remained in total darkness for 88 days, the other 126 days. Each guessed how long they could remain in darkness and were off by months. One took what he thought was a short nap only to discover he'd slept for thirty hours. Darkness is disorienting.

The people of God found themselves in the darkness of impending exile. They waited, unsure of what would take place. The prophet Isaiah used darkness as a metaphor for their disorientation and as a way of speaking about God's judgment (Isaiah 8:22). Previously, the Egyptians had been visited with darkness as a plague (Exodus 10:21–29). Now Israel found herself in darkness.

But a light would come. "The people walking in darkness have seen a great light; on those living in the land of deep darkness a light has dawned" (Isaiah 9:2). Oppression would be broken, disorientation would end. A Child would come to change everything and bring about a new day—a day of forgiveness and freedom (v. 6).

Jesus did come! And although the darkness of the world can be disorienting, may we experience the comfort of the forgiveness, freedom, and light found in Christ.

LIFE MOMENT

How appealing does it sound to you to take a sleep study in a pitch-dark cave?

GOD MOMENT

In what way does the Savior rescue you from the darkness that surrounds us in our world?

> *A Child would come to change everything.*

97

True Worshipers

John 4:19-26

True worshipers will worship the Father
in the Spirit and in truth.

John 4:23

She finally had the chance to visit the church. Inside, in the deepest part of the basement, she reached the small cave or grotto. Candles filled the narrow space and hanging lamps illuminated a corner of the floor. There it was—a fourteen-pointed silver star, covering a raised bit of the marble floor. She was in Bethlehem's Grotto of the Nativity—the place marking the spot where according to tradition Christ was born. Yet the writer Annie Dillard felt less than impressed, realizing God was much bigger than that spot.

Still, such places have always held great significance in our faith stories. Another such place is mentioned in the conversation between Jesus and the woman at the well—the mountain where her "ancestors worshiped" (John 4:20), referring to Mount Gerizim (see Deuteronomy 11:29). It was sacred to the Samaritans, who contrasted it to the Jewish insistence that Jerusalem was where true worship occurred (v. 20). However, Jesus declared the time had arrived when worship was no longer specific to a place, but a Person: "the true worshipers will worship the Father in the Spirit and in truth" (v. 23). The woman declared her faith in the Messiah, but she didn't realize she was talking to Him. "Then Jesus declared, 'I, the one speaking to you—I am he'" (v. 26).

God isn't limited to any mountain or physical space. He's present with us everywhere. The true pilgrimage we make each day is to approach His throne as we boldly say, "Our Father," and He is there.

LIFE MOMENT

If you had the chance to go to Israel, what would be one place on your "Don't miss" agenda?

GOD MOMENT

How often do you make a "pilgrimage" with Jesus by reading Scripture, praying, and spending time with Him? Daily, weekly, monthly?

> *God isn't limited to any mountain or physical space.*

98

My Help!

Psalm 121

My help comes from the LORD, the Maker of heaven and earth.

Psalm 121:2

Have you ever heard the folks from the Brooklyn Tabernacle Choir? Amazing voices and great gospel songs! One example is their recording from Psalm 121 titled "My Help."

Psalm 121 begins with a personal confession of faith in the Lord, who brought all things into existence, and He was the source of the psalmist's help (vv. 1–2). Just what did this mean? Stability (v. 3), around-the-clock care (vv. 3–4), constant presence and protection (vv. 5–6), and preservation from all kinds of evil for time and eternity (vv. 7–8).

Taking their cues from Scripture, God's people through the ages have identified the Lord as their source of "help" through their songs. They have lifted their voices with others who have sung a soulful rendition of Charles Wesley's, "Father, I stretch my hands to Thee, no other help I know; if Thou withdraw Thyself from me, ah! whither shall I go." The great reformer Martin Luther got it right when he penned these words: "A mighty fortress is our God, a bulwark never failing; our helper He amid the flood of mortal ills prevailing."

At times, do you feel alone? Forsaken? Overwhelmed? Ponder the lyrics of Psalm 121. Allow these words to fill your soul with faith and courage. You're not alone, so don't try to do life on your own. Rather, rejoice in the earthly and eternal care of God as demonstrated in the life, death, resurrection, and ascension of the Lord Jesus Christ. And whatever the next steps, take them with His help.

LIFE MOMENT

What hymn has special meaning to you?

GOD MOMENT

Think about Psalm 121:2. The One who created the universe cares for the individual person. How does that idea impact your thinking?

> *You're not alone, so don't try
> to do life on your own.*

99

The True Servant

Philippians 2:6-11

Being found in appearance as a man, [Jesus] humbled himself
by becoming obedient to death—even death on a cross!
Philippians 2:8

I n 27 BC, the Roman ruler Octavian came before the Senate to lay
down his powers. He'd won a civil war, become the sole ruler of that
region of the world, and was functioning like an emperor. Yet he knew
such power was viewed suspiciously. So Octavian renounced his powers before the Senate, vowing to simply be an appointed official. Their
response? The Roman Senate honored the ruler by crowning him with a
civic crown and naming him the servant of the Roman people. He was
also given the name Augustus—the "great one."

Paul wrote of Jesus emptying himself and taking on the form of a
servant. Augustus appeared to do the same. Or had he? Augustus only
acted like he was surrendering his power, but he was doing it for his own
gain. Jesus "humbled himself by becoming obedient to death—even
death on a cross!" (Philippians 2:8). Death on a Roman cross was the
worst form of humiliation and shame.

Today, a primary reason people praise "servant leadership" as a virtue
is because of Jesus. Humility wasn't a Greek or Roman virtue. Because
Jesus died on the cross for us, He's the true Servant. He's the true Savior.

Christ became a servant in order to save us. He "made himself nothing" (v. 7) so that we could receive something truly great—the gift of salvation and eternal life.

LIFE MOMENT

When have you had to humble yourself to serve someone else?

GOD MOMENT

Think for a moment about Jesus's humility. How can you best put into words the humility of the God of the universe in His relationship to you?

> *Because Jesus died on the cross for us,*
> *He's the true Servant. He's the true Savior.*

100

Follow Jesus into the Unknown

Mark 3:13-19

"Come, follow me," Jesus said, . . . At once
they left their nets and followed Him.

Mark 1:17-18

When the United States launched its space program in 1958, seven men were chosen to become the first astronauts. Imagine the excitement of Scott Carpenter, Gordon Cooper, John Glenn, Gus Grissom, Walter Schirra, Alan Shepard, and Deke Slayton. They were selected to go where no one had ever gone before.

Yet, as astronauts they knew they would face unforeseen dangers, challenges, and trials. Each of them realized that the thrill of being chosen was tempered with the fear of the unknown future.

Imagine another set of men who were chosen for an important mission: the twelve apostles Jesus chose one day on a mountainside near the Sea of Galilee. These men left behind their occupations and families to dedicate themselves to this radical new teacher. They didn't know what kind of political, religious, or financial challenges they would face. Yet they followed Jesus.

Jesus asks the same of His people today. He asks each of us to follow Him, to love Him, to obey Him, and to tell others about Him. Like the apostles, we don't know what our commitment to Jesus might bring.

Lord, help us to follow you faithfully and to trust you completely with our future.

LIFE MOMENT

What was the greatest challenge you were ever chosen to accept? How did you do?

GOD MOMENT

What might cause us to balk at God's challenges to us? Have you ever felt God's call to do something but were reluctant—scared, actually—to follow through?

> The Twelve didn't know what kind of political, religious, or financial challenges they would face. Yet they followed Jesus.

CONTRIBUTORS

James Banks
John Blase
Amy Boucher Pye
Dave Branon
Winn Collier
Bill Crowder
Mart DeHaan
Tim Gustafson
Kirsten Holmberg
Adam Holz
Arthur Jackson
Julie Ackerman Link
Glenn Packiam
Patricia Raybon
David Roper
Lisa M. Samra
Mike Wittmer

To learn more about the writers of *Our Daily Bread*,
visit odb.org/all-authors.

GENERAL EDITOR

Dave Branon retired in 2021 after a forty-year career as a writer and editor with Our Daily Bread Ministries. Dave has written for the *Our Daily Bread* devotional since 1988—more than 1,200 articles. He has also written 20 books, which include *Beyond the Valley: Finding Hope in Life's Losses* and *Lands of the Bible Today*. He and his wife, Sue, who have four children and eight grandchildren, live in Grand Rapids, Michigan.